Ruby Recipes

A Problem-Solution Approach

■ ■ ■

Malay Mandal

Apress®

Ruby Recipes: A Problem-Solution Approach

Malay Mandal
New South Wales, Australia

ISBN-13 (pbk): 978-1-4842-2468-7   ISBN-13 (electronic): 978-1-4842-2469-4
DOI 10.1007/978-1-4842-2469-4

Library of Congress Control Number: 2016960330

Managing Director: Welmoed Spahr
Lead Editor: Celestin Suresh John
Technical Reviewer: Unmesh Gundecha
Editorial Board: Steve Anglin, Pramila Balan, Laura Berendson, Aaron Black,
    Louise Corrigan, Jonathan Gennick, Robert Hutchinson, Celestin Suresh John,
    Nikhil Karkal, James Markham, Susan McDermott, Matthew Moodie, Natalie Pao,
    Gwenan Spearing
Coordinating Editor: Prachi Mehta
Copy Editor: Kim Burton-Weisman
Compositor: SPi Global
Indexer: SPi Global
Artist: SPi Global

Distributed to the book trade worldwide by Springer Science+Business Media New York, 233 Spring Street, 6th Floor, New York, NY 10013. Phone 1-800-SPRINGER, fax (201) 348-4505, e-mail orders-ny@springer-sbm.com, or visit www.springeronline.com. Apress Media, LLC is a California LLC and the sole member (owner) is Springer Science + Business Media Finance Inc (SSBM Finance Inc). SSBM Finance Inc is a **Delaware** corporation.

For information on translations, please e-mail rights@apress.com, or visit www.apress.com.

Apress and friends of ED books may be purchased in bulk for academic, corporate, or promotional use. eBook versions and licenses are also available for most titles. For more information, reference our Special Bulk Sales–eBook Licensing web page at www.apress.com/bulk-sales.

Any source code or other supplementary materials referenced by the author in this text are available to readers at www.apress.com. For detailed information about how to locate your book's source code, go to www.apress.com/source-code/. Readers can also access source code at SpringerLink in the Supplementary Material section for each chapter.

Printed on acid-free paper

Dedicated to my mother for all her support and concern.

Contents at a Glance

Contents

About the Author

Malay Mandal is a postgraduate mechanical engineer by qualification, but built a career in software engineering instead. He has worked with software in a professional capacity for more than 22 years. In his spare time, he sometimes delves into diverse topics of software technologies. He has worked across multiple languages and technologies, including client-server, RDBMS, Java, and Scala. He has tried many different things over the years; developing Android apps, and authoring and publishing books are some of his more recent endeavors.

Acknowledgments

Thanks to Jayati (my wife) for supplying all the cups of coffee. Sometimes I badly needed them.

Thanks to Suresh John Celestin (of Apress) for his support in this endeavor.

Thanks to the technical reviewers for their thoughtful suggestions.

Introduction

Target audience

```
if ((someone knows at least one computer language
and
wants to have a quick go at Ruby
or
wants to quickly get up and running with Ruby for some programming tasks,
without learning all the language features
or
wants to pick up a computer language well enough (rather quickly) to develop
programs to accomplish certain tasks,
or
is seeking a computer language where simple development is rather quick and
lucid
))
he can make good use of the book

/* It is a reasonably quick (and possibly interesting) read and comes with a
lot of ready code */
```

A Few Things About the Book

Ruby refers to the programming language (not a gemstone); that much you might have figured out already.

Quite often in life, we may need to learn something reasonably well, but do not need to master it. Consider my cooking for example.

I hope you would have guessed by now what kind of a cook I am. Although some people may consider it fortunate that quite often I am the sole consumer of my cooking.

Although the book name contains the word "Recipes," rest assured, it has nothing to do with my cooking.

The teaching in this book revolves around demonstrable examples and case studies. It is supposed to have somewhat quick-and-easy solutions. (Although what is considered "quick" and what is considered "easy" is quite subjective).

And as far as quick and easy solutions go, it may get you on your feet (figuratively speaking) and help you get going, (rather steadily one may hope), in the journey of Ruby programming.

This is not a complete treatise on all the features of Ruby language, but it discusses enough (perhaps more than enough) to accomplish a lot of simple-to-intermediate-level tasks that a programmer or analyst (or even people in another profession) may have a need to accomplish, either occasionally or on a day-to-day basis.

The fact that it is not a complete treatise of the language has its obvious merits and demerits. One of the demerits being that it won't make you an expert of the language. You will need further exploration if being an expert is your goal. The obvious merit is that you can finish it quickly and possibly without much rigorous mental effort. (And as a side effect, it is lesser in volume and thus costs less than what it otherwise would).

Instead of a "big bang" approach (of describing all the syntax first, and then starting the actual tasks), at least at the initial part of the book, elements have been introduced in short increments, usually accompanied by examples. In my experience, that often makes for interesting reading. Although that may mean that all related concepts are not strictly grouped together.

This book does not discuss Rails and it does not explore the object-oriented side of Ruby. In fact, it does not cover class definition in Ruby. But it does cover many of the language elements that cater to many day-to-day programming needs. In particular, it has good coverage of basic variables, operators, control flow, collections, and regular expressions.

This version is based upon Ruby 2.3.1, which is latest stable version as of today (today being October 3, 2016). However, since the bulk of the code uses rather simple features of the language, it is likely that it would run without any modification for many Ruby versions to come. If you are using it far into the future of this date, and you need to use a piece of code for your task, my advice is to try it as it is on your current version, prior to trying to upgrading the code (chances are that you won't have to upgrade).

At times, it was a bit of hard work, but I also enjoyed writing it. I hope that reading the book is an enjoyable experience for you as well.

About the Format of the Book

At times, this book deviates from the usual format of Apress Recipe books. Instead of a Problem/Solution/How It Works kind of template, sometimes the discussion digresses, in some depth, to discuss a particular topic.

As I wrote the book, I sometimes let it develop (as it were) at its own pace and rhythm, and let certain things come out rather naturally. Not wanting to force-fit many parts of the book, I intended to conform to the template, after the fact. This was partly because it is not always easy to change the form of a creation after it has developed completely, and partly because I felt that in many cases, the actual flow of discussion, as it stood, would be more fit for ready absorption, rather than trying to force-fit it into a template.

In my view, this digression from formatting does not take away from the readability of the book. If anything, I believe it adds to it.

But I leave it up to you to see for yourself and come to your own conclusion.

Why Ruby?

The brief answer is "power and ease."

A more detailed answer is that Ruby is a full-fledged programming language. That is where the "power" comes in.

It comes with language constructs, such as powerful control flow statements like for and while, collection structures like arrays and hashes, scoping of variables, and even some powerful functional programming features, such as lambda, which was introduced in Ruby long before it was introduced in Java. (Contrast that with a shell scripting environment, where your choices of constructs are far more limited).

Although what is easy and what is difficult is subjective, the easy part, in my view, is (at least) twofold.

First, it can run like an interpreted script (it can also be compiled but that is not the point here) without any compilation, like a series of statements. The beauty of that is a reduced boilerplate and a reduced run cycle (need not compile and then run). A Hello World program in Ruby can be written in one line (and without squeezing multiple statements to reduce line count). And that can be run with a single command (no separate compilation). Contrast that with a Java Hello World code, which would, at the minimum, require a class and a main method. And also requires compilation.

The other part of the ease is the somewhat English-like lucid syntax of the language. (As an aside, this was my initial point of attraction to the language). Consider the following statement:

```
print "a is negative" unless a >= 0
```

This is a valid statement in Ruby. In my long experience as a software engineer, I have not known many languages that are this English-like out of the box.

For an even more detailed answer, you should read the book and decide for yourself.

Conventions and Assumptions

The (command line) commands are usually shown, enclosed by single quotes (e.g., 'ruby -v') to distinguish the exact command from other part of the text. The actual command, however, is the inside of the quotes without the single quotes. The same applies to name of directories or files in many places. (e.g., a file mentioned as 'hello.rb' is a file named like that, without the enclosing single quotes).

Text output or data input, especially while being described within textual description (e.g., "prints 'Hello World' in the terminal"), may describe the piece of output within single quotes, where the single quotes are not part of the output, but a convenient means to separate the exact output text, from the surrounding descriptions.

Sometimes a part of terminal input and output is replicated in the book, for example:

```
=>ruby -v
```

ruby 2.3.1p112 (2016-04-26 revision 54768) [x86_64-darwin13]

Here, the initial '=>' is the operating system prompt and not part of the actual command. (in your machine, the prompt may be set up differently, e.g., 'C:\test>').

Pieces of code are usually printed in a separate font and / or style.

Sometimes evaluation of an expression, or a String when printed and such like (evaluated values) are written after the expression following a '=>' sign. This is not part of the language but just shorthand used in the book for translates into, for example:

```
2 + 3 * 5 => 17
```

One or more lines of code (or input/output data) when given by itself (i.e., not inline within part of a textual description, may be separated by one blank line each at the beginning and end of the piece. Those blank lines are not part of the actual code or data.

Sometimes, when an output is mentioned, only the visible character part may be mentioned (and the trailing newline is omitted from the description, even though that may be part of the output).

Pieces of code and input and output data displayed in the book may be reformatted (for instance, to beautify for better printing/display). Trailing spaces, new lines, indentations and such, may be added or removed. But even in such cases, code should still be working code and data and format should be correct and meaningful for the context.

Quite often in the book, a colloquial style has been used, which might have expressions like "Let's write," or "Let's do." This is, as if the reader is with me, and we are going through the exercise together. That is usually not the case. This, however, is a style of writing, and probably adds to the ease of understanding and to the ease of explaining.

In any part, when the effect of a code run is described in a way like "it should produce" or "you will get," it is assumed that compatible version of Ruby is properly set up and running on your PC, and there is no other issues—that is, the code is being run successfully (apart from the cases when the discussion specifies that it would result in an exception). If the installation or environment setup is incorrect, then that likely would not be the case.

CHAPTER 1

■ ■ ■

A Taste of Ruby

"To err is human, but to really foul things up you need a computer."

—Paul R. Ehrlich

The hammer is still in fashion. Don't get me wrong. I am not here to make a fashion statement (at least not in the conventional way). And I have not seen any fashion parade where any of the models were carrying a hammer.

We have made a lot of advancement in science and technology. The invention of the wheel was a fundamental one. There were steam engines, solar cells, televisions, machine guns, and now there are smartphones.

A hammer is a tool. It has been around far longer than the smartphone and it has contributed to human advancement by a far greater degree. And I would think, unless a suitable alternative is found, a world without hammers would be far less livable than a world without smartphones (Actually, it may be argued whether we would be better off in a world without smartphones).

So, as it happens, the hammer is still in fashion as a tool.

But why am I talking about hammers in a computer programming book?

Small Task, Big Impact

As you might have guessed, it was more in a metaphorical sense that I started the discussion on hammers. It is a seemingly simple tool, but indispensable in many tasks.

In my 20 years (approximately) of professional software development experience, I often found it handy to write small scripts to parse text and/or perform other operations, such classifying files into different directories. In typical IT job ads, among the crowd of big-name software tools and languages, you do not usually find a mention of this particular skill. But in some cases it is useful and in other cases it is very useful. The hammer is a

Electronic supplementary material The online version of this chapter (doi:10.1007/978-1-4842-2469-4_1) contains supplementary material, which is available to authorized users.

M. Mandal, *Ruby Recipes*, DOI 10.1007/978-1-4842-2469-4_1

simple but effective tool. Ruby, particularly Ruby scripting, can also be used very effectively to accomplish a lot of tasks (and is perhaps considered simple in some perspectives—especially based on the features that are used and the way that they are used).

Development Environment Installation

In order to have a real taste of a language, you need to have an environment where you can play with it. The following sections are brief discussions on installation on the Mac and Windows.

If you are reading this book somewhat far into the future after it was published, you should start with a Google search on "Ruby installation" or "installing Ruby" to find the official Ruby installation page.

As of today, the installation page is at

```
https://www.ruby-lang.org/en/documentation/installation/
```

It has information sources and links to help with Ruby installation in various platforms.

Windows

On the Ruby installation page mentioned earlier, there is a link for RubyInstaller, which takes you to the download page. Alternatively, you can go directly to `http://rubyinstaller.org/downloads/` and download the latest version. The current version is 2.3.1.

The installer is really an `.exe` file; the installation instruction for RubyInstaller on the `ruby-lang.org` installation page of is rather short and sweet: *Just download it, run it, and you are done!*

The installation should be rather like usual Windows software installations. To check that it was properly installed and is available in the path, open a command prompt, and issue this command:

```
ruby -v
```

This should produce a meaningful message regarding the Ruby version (installed and available in path), and possibly a revision date, and the target architecture of the version. For example:

```
ruby 2.3.1p112 (2016-04-26 revision 54768) [x64-mingw32]
```

Mac

On the Mac it is slightly trickier.

It is possible that your Mac already has Ruby installed. If you open a terminal and issue the `ruby -v` command, you may see something like this:

```
=>ruby -v
ruby 2.0.0p481 (2014-05-08 revision 45883) [universal.x86_64-darwin13]
```

The code used in this book, although checked against version 2.3.1, will very likely run on a few older versions (although this is not guaranteed). So you may wish to proceed with the current version (if any) that you have installed (and try upgrading it later, if required).

If your version is older than your target working version, you can upgrade Ruby on your Mac. (The commands are given as follows, so you will not probably need to look it up on the web page, but in case you are interested: on recent Mac operating systems, a good way to upgrade or install Ruby is to follow https://gorails.com/setup/osx/ and choose the page for your Mac operating system version.

Although this page has instructions installing Rails, for the purpose of this book, you only need the first two steps:

1. Install Homebrew.

2. Install Ruby.

Make sure that you are connected to the Internet (and you need to have admin rights on your machine).

The following is the command for installing Homebrew, which helps install and compile software packages easily from the source:

```
ruby -e "$(curl -fsSL https://raw.githubusercontent.com/Homebrew/install/
master/install)"
```

These are the commands for Ruby installation:

```
brew install rbenv ruby-build
rbenv install 2.3.1
rbenv global 2.3.1
```

Check your Ruby installation by running this:

```
=>ruby -v
ruby 2.3.1p112 (2016-04-26 revision 54768) [x86_64-darwin13]
```

Add the following line to your .profile or .bash_profile file:

```
echo 'if which rbenv > /dev/null; then eval "$(rbenv init -)"; fi' >>
~/.bash_profile
```

This should load the correct Ruby version every time that you open a new terminal.

Close the terminal, open a new one, and check (with the ruby -v command) that the correct version is indeed available.

1.1 The First Recipe: aka Hello World

By now, hopefully, your development environment is up and running, and the ruby command is available in the path. It's time to have a first go at real Ruby programming. And as a (somewhat unofficial) tradition of programming language learning, let's start with the Hello World program.

In order to structure the exercises better, you can create a root directory for the book's code, somewhere on your machine. Suppose the directory is named exer and it is created directly under your home directory (it could be elsewhere also).

Under the exer directory, a separate directory can be created for each chapter (such as chap01 for the first chapter, and so on). The coding for a chapter may be kept and run directly from the chapter directory (unless there is a specific need to separate code or data files, for one or more specific exercises, in which case the chapter directory may have subdirectories).

So for now, this is the suggested structure:

```
exer
            /chap01
            /chap02
```

Problem

You want to create code in Ruby that prints 'Hello World' (without the single quotes) to the terminal.

Solution

Open a terminal/command prompt and go to this chapter's directory. Create a file named hello.rb. Write a single line of code in the file, as follows.

```
puts "Hello World"
```

Save and close the file. In the command prompt, type the following command.

```
ruby hello.rb
```

Press Return. This should print 'Hello World' in the terminal/console.

How It Works

If you are disappointed that this is too easy—don't be! In fact, that is one of the main reasons why Ruby may considered a good tool to use. It's too easy.

But easy as it may be, if this is your very first exposure to Ruby programming, you may wish to note a few things.

Running a program is done with the ruby command, with the program's file name as the *first argument*. The program itself may take its own arguments, which follow the program's file name. More on this later.

The program file extension is immaterial. By convention, the extension is .rb, but any extension is really OK. You can test this by copying the hello.rb file to another file named hello.txt. Issue the ruby hello.txt command—and the result should still be the same.

One way to print a string to the console is by using the puts function, followed by the string to be printed within in double quotes, as an argument. Notice that I wrote *one way to*. There are other ways to achieve same effect. For one, in this case, the double quotes could safely be replaced by single quotes, and it would still work (i.e., puts 'Hello World' instead of puts "Hello World").

Parentheses in a method call omitted. Note that for the function puts, the argument (the 'Hello World' string) is not enclosed in parentheses. Parentheses in the method argument are quite often (but not in all cases) optional (another goody of the Ruby language, you might say). It is a liberty that you cannot enjoy with many other programming languages. The fact that it is optional can be readily verified by actually putting the parentheses (i.e., puts("Hello World") instead of puts "Hello World") in the code, and trying to run it. It should work equally well.

■ **Note**   If you use parentheses, make it a practice not to have many spaces between the function name and the opening parentheses. In some situations, such a space may cause syntax error.

No semicolon. The statement does not end in a semicolon. Again, this is optional in many cases, including where you have only one statement in a line.

1.2 Does It Cost Anything to Say Hello?

It may not seem like much in retrospect, but assuming you started from scratch (to set up the environment, etc.), the first Hello said in this new language (assuming it is new for you) did come at a certain cost in terms of time and effort. (And that without considering the amount of energy your computer consumed in the process).

But from another perspective, consider how much time (although it is not the same for each individual) and effort it takes for a human baby to say "Hello" clearly for the first time in his native language.

In that sense, it can be considered a very quick first expression in a new language.

While we are at it, you may want to see some basic numeracy expressed in Ruby and pick up a few more points regarding the language.

Problem

You want to add 2 and 2 together and print the result on a console.

Solution

If your first instinct is to just add 2 and 2, and use puts to print it directly—that is, just a single line of code, like the following, you are spot on.

```
puts 2 + 2
```

It does the trick.

```
=>ruby sum.rb
4
```

How It Works

As you might have noticed, puts can work with non-strings. (It actually implicitly converts non-string arguments to strings). In general, it is not the case that a function, which expects string arguments, works seamlessly with other type of arguments by converting the argument to a string. (In some computer languages, a similar function for printing output to console would fail if you provide a non-string argument.)

It is a no-brainer that multiplication of two integers can work very similarly.

The following prints a 6.

```
puts 2 * 3
```

The code that follows here, however, prints a 13.

```
puts 2 + 2 + 3 * 3
```

The expression '2 + 2 + 3 * 3', which results in '13' may give you some idea about the operator precedence in Ruby. It works predictably similar to many other programming languages in regards to numerical expression. But this chapter is more about providing you with a taste of Ruby, so a detailed discussion on operator precedence is rather out of place right now.

1.3 Sherlock Holmes and Learning

You might have heard or read about Sherlock Holmes, the great detective. He was not a real character, but that's beside the point. The story of Sherlock Holmes was so inspiring that (although the original publication of the last tale appeared in 1927) even in recent times, TV series have been made based on the theme.

Sherlock Holmes was a keen observer and a deductionist. He observed things in great detail; detail that might have eluded others in the same spot. But that is perhaps not the only point about his observation.

He would observe things that were pertinent to the case.

There is a great story, although I suspect it was not written by Sir Arthur Conan Doyle, the creator of the Sherlock Holmes character. I will retell the story in my own way.

One day Holmes and Watson went on a camping trip. They put up their tent in the early afternoon. They enjoyed some coffee, done a bit of fishing, and took a stroll. As the darkness fell, they sat around the camp fire with steins of beer in their hands. They talked about this and that, and as usual, got into a fierce argument every now and then. As night fell, they had an early dinner and went to sleep. In the wee hours of the night, Watson woke up, prodded by a nudge from Holmes. The conversation that took place between them went somewhat like this:

Holmes: "Watson, get up. Look into the sky and tell me what you see."

Watson: "I see a clear blue sky and a lot of stars."

Holmes: "And what does that tell you?"

Watson: "That the night sky is beautiful. So beautiful that it can inspire one to be a poet or an artist. That there are billions of starts in the universe and we are rather insignificant on the astronomical scale. I can also predict with a degree of certainty that tomorrow is going to be a fine day."

Holmes: "Hmmm."

Watson: "Anything I have missed in particular?"

Holmes: "Our tent has been stolen."

The point I am trying to make is, Holmes not only observes, but observes particularly from the point of view that is important in the context. (In his case, the typical context was solving a crime). He observes contextually.

What relevance does that have to learning? More specifically, what is the relation of contextual observation to learning a programming language?

To answer that in a rather decorated fashion, let us consider the following problem.

Problem

You want to assign a value to a variable in Ruby.

Solution

Create file called `vari.rb` and add the following lines.

```
a = 1
b = 2.5
c = "three"
d = 4
e = a + d
```

Save and close the file, and try to run it. It does not give any error, because all of these are valid assignments in Ruby.

How It Works

Now, get into Sherlock Holmes mode. What do you observe?

On the outset, those are three lines of code with some variable names on the left (equal signs) and some values on the right.

It is also perhaps a no-brainer that a is an integer (or a `Fixnum` in Ruby), b is a float, and c is a string.

What is really interesting, however, is that the *variable type need not be declared in Ruby*. It also cannot be declared; the only way is to make a type class, if you wish to make type declarations for variables (actually, objects in that case). This (non-declaration of variable types) is a core Ruby feature.

Not only that, if you add a sixth line (b = "Hello") to the vari.rb file, the entire code is as follows.

```
a = 1
b = 2.5
c = "three"
d = 4
e = a + d
b = "Hello"
```

If you then save and run it, it would still be OK. This means that in addition to the fact that types of variables are not declared, but *the same variable may take up different types of values at different times in the course of the program.* Ruby is a dynamically typed language.

Not being explicit with variable types and changing it dynamically within the program's lifetime has its disadvantages (especially from a robustness point of view). But for small code (scripts are usually smaller than a full-fledged web application for instance), it may not be such a serious issue. And it saves some time (less typing) if you don't have to declare the types.

1.4 1 2 3 4, 1 2 3 4

How do you repeat things in a loop in Ruby?

There are several ways actually. Let's start with a problem.

Problem

You want to print 1 to 10 (on separate lines) in a loop.

Solution

Create a fortest.rb file in the chap01 folder. Open and write the following three lines of code.

```
for i in 1..10
        puts i
end
```

Save and close the file. When you run it, it should produce the desired result.

```
=>ruby fortest.rb
1
2
3
4
```

```
5
6
7
8
9
10
```

How It Works

If you know some other programming language, chances are that you may have come across code for a for loop, which is remarkably similar to the following.

```
for (int i = 1; i <= 10; i++)
        System.out.println("" + i);
```

If you have not come across such code in the past, consider it a piece of pseudo code for the benefit of our discussion. In the preceding (non-Ruby) code, apart from the lack of semicolons and such, which has already been discussed, note the following.

- *Implicit type definition*: The i variable did not require to be defined as an int (for Ruby this is actually Fixnum type not int).

- *Implicit step size*: An increment of i at each step, even when it is 1, has to be explicit (e.g., i++), but not so in Ruby. (Although if the step was not one in this case, it would no longer be implicit, even in Ruby).

- *The* end *keyword for the end of the block*: The block of code ends in the end keyword.

Note that the program could have been written in a single line, like this:

```
for i in 1..10; puts i; end
```

(And this is not particular to Ruby. Many programming languages would allow putting multiple statements in one line, provided they are separated with the appropriate statement end markers. However, it is usually not a good programming practice to squeeze multiple statements on one line).

The earlier (multiline) form of for statement shows that *not only for simple statements, but even for control structures such as* for, *a line break can act as a statement terminator/condition separator*. The overall condition of the for was finished in the first line and the actual work in the loop started on the second line.

Note that although it is redundant, you can put semicolons at the end of statements—even when they occur by themselves in the line. (But why should you?)

Thus the following is valid code.

```
for i in 1..5;
        puts i;
        puts i * 2;
end;
```

Note that since a for loop signifies a code block, it is quite natural to use multiple statements within it, when required.

Interactive Ruby Shell

Ruby comes with an interactive Ruby shell. The command, not surprisingly, is named irb.

If you type the command in your terminal/command prompt, and then press the Return key, the prompt will change.

```
=>irb
irb(main):001:0>
```

This is a shell that you can run Ruby code directly, line by line (or block by block), and it will evaluate on the fly. The following shows some interaction.

```
irb(main):001:0> a = 2 + 2
=> 4
irb(main):002:0> 2 + 2
=> 4
irb(main):003:0> b = 3
=> 3
irb(main):004:0> a + b
=> 7
irb(main):005:0> for i in 1..5
irb(main):006:1> puts i
irb(main):007:1> end
1
2
3
4
5
=> 1..5
irb(main):008:0>
```

Note that the for loop waited for the entire block to finish before executing. In cases where the line itself is a complete command, it evaluates immediately after the line.

■ **Note**   Control+D lets you exit from the shell.

In this book, irb is used for quick demonstrations of certain features (hence, you will see more of it). It is a tool that is available at your disposal for quick verification or quick evaluation of certain things (e.g., for checking the validity of a statement syntax-wise).

You can also use it as a simple calculator.

```
=>irb
irb(main):001:0> 26 * 26
=> 676
```

Summary

Assuming that you are new to it, you have had your first taste of the Ruby language; hopefully, you have liked it thus far.

Apart from a brief discussion on installation, this chapter discussed

- how to run a Ruby program file from console

- how to print strings and variable values to the console

- some simple operators

- variable declaration (or lack thereof) and assignments

- a looping mechanism

- the interactive Ruby shell

Here is a quick recapitulation of some commands and code.

```
ruby hello.rb
puts "Hello World"
puts 2 + 2
a = 1
b = 2.5
for i in 1..10
        puts i
end
```

What has been discussed so far should be good enough for you to write some simple programs. The following is a set of exercises. These are not essential for learning, but you may wish to try them nevertheless. The solutions are in the appendix.

Exercises

Exercise 1.1

Write a program to calculate the sum of the square of the first ten positive integers (1 to 10).

Exercise 1.2

Write a program to calculate the factorial of 6 (for positive integers, the factorial of a number is the product of all numbers, starting from 1 and up to and including that number. For example, the factorial of 3 = 1 * 2 * 3 (= 6)).

Exercise 1.3

Fibonacci numbers are defined as a series of integers, where any number, from the third number onward, is the sum of its immediate two predecessors. (Of course, the initial two numbers have to be given, which can be taken as 0 and 1 in our case). So the series should be 0,1,1,2,3,5,.... Write code to print the first ten Fibonacci numbers after the initial 0 and 1 (the initial 0 and 1 need not be printed by this program).

CHAPTER 2

■ ■ ■

Working with Files and Strings

This chapter contains recipes for working with files and strings. I'll start, however, with a section on the theory of manipulating strings. It is designed to make you aware of certain ways of manipulating strings (and to give you some useful tools).

Manipulating Strings

The Ruby String class has plenty of methods. Following a *somewhat* "minimalist knowledge" approach (i.e., knowing only as much as is required), only some functions are discussed in this section. Note that the methods discussed here usually return a copy of the part of / modified version original string (as required) and do not modify the original string.

length or size

The length method is used to get the size (in characters) of the string. (The same can be achieved by using the size function.)

```
"abcd".length => 4
```

empty?

The empty? method returns true if the string is empty; otherwise, it is false.

```
irb(main):001:0> "hello".empty?
=> false
irb(main):002:0> "".empty?
=> true
```

© Malay Mandal 2016
M. Mandal, *Ruby Recipes*, DOI 10.1007/978-1-4842-2469-4_2

strip

`strip` removes the leading and trailing whitespace (and trailing NUL) characters.

```
"   hello   " => "hello"
```

The functions `lstrip` or `rstrip` may be used for removing spaces only from left or right side.

<<

`<<` is used for concatenation.

```
irb(main):007:0> a = "hello"
=> "hello"
irb(main):008:0> a << "world"
=> "helloworld"
```

<=>

`<=>` compares two strings. It returns –1, 0, or 1 based on whether the first string is lesser than, equal to, or greater than the second.

```
irb(main):009:0> "hello" <=> "world"
=> -1
irb(main):011:0> 'ddd' <=> 'ccc'
=> 1
```

capitalize

`capitalize` returns a copy with the first letter capitalized and the rest in lowercase. (There are quite a few functions in Ruby's `String` class that deal with the cases of letters.)

```
"hello".capitalize => "Hello"
"Hello".capitalize => "Hello"
"HELLO".capitalize => "Hello"
```

downcase and upcase

As the names suggest, `downcase` and `upcase` return strings with the case converted.

```
irb(main):003:0> "Hello".downcase
=> "hello"
irb(main):004:0> "Hello".upcase
=> "HELLO"
```

chars

chars returns an array corresponding to the characters in the string.

```
irb(main):001:0> "abracadabra".chars
=> ["a", "b", "r", "a", "c", "a", "d", "a", "b", "r", "a"]
```

index

index is the index of the first occurrence of a character, substring, or pattern in a string. It returns *nil* if not found.

```
"Hello".index('e') => 1
```

index can also start from an offset position in order to look for the second index position (the third character) onward from a string and pass the index position (offset) as the second argument.

```
irb(main):001:0> "Hello".index('e',1)
=> 1
irb(main):002:0> "Hello".index('e',2)
=> nil
```

In the latter case, 'e' does not occur on or after the second index (character 3).

insert

insert inserts one given string into another, prior to the given index position.

```
irb(main):006:0> "abraabra".insert(4,'cad')
=> "abracadabra"
```

delete

delete returns a new string with characters deleted, as specified. It has a few different forms.

```
irb(main):007:0> "hello".delete "l"          #delete any 'l' from "hello"
=> "heo"
irb(main):008:0> "hello".delete "lo"         #delete any 'l' or 'o'
=> "he"
irb(main):009:0> "hello".delete "aeiou", "^e"   #delete any of 'a','e',
                                                 'i','o','u' except 'e'
=> "hell"
irb(main):010:0> "hello".delete "ek-m"          #delete any 'e' or any of
                                                 'k' to 'm'
=> "ho"
```

include?

include? returns a Boolean that indicates whether the argument string is part of the first string.

```
irb(main):005:0> "Hello world".include?("world")
=> true
```

slice

slice returns part of the string (somewhat like substring function) or returns nil. *Note that this function has many forms, including one that returns int. Only one form is discussed in this section.*

```
<String>.slice(start index,length), e.g.
"hello".slice(1,3) => "ell"
```

count

count counts the given character(s). It has a few different forms.

```
irb(main):001:0> "hello".count('l') # how many 'l' in "hello"
=> 2
irb(main):002:0> "hello".count('lo') # how many 'l' or 'o' in "hello"
=> 3
irb(main):003:0> "hello".count('a-h') # how many characters within the range
a to h
=> 2
irb(main):004:0> "hello".count('^a-h') # how many characters not within the
range a to h
=> 3
```

partition

partition partitions a string into array of strings based on (the first occurrence of) a given character or pattern.

```
irb(main):012:0> "hello".partition('l')
=> ["he", "l", "lo"]
```

tr

tr transforms a string by replacing some characters with others, as specified. It has multiple forms.

```
irb(main):015:0> "hello".tr('l','m')
=> "hemmo"
irb(main):016:0> "hello".tr('a-f','x')
=> "hxllo"
```

reverse

reverse returns the reverse of the string.

```
irb(main):017:0> "hello".reverse
=> "olleh"
```

sub (and gsub)

sub and gsub have more than one form. One form is discussed in this section; it substitutes specified parts of the string with a replacement. It works with patterns; however, patterns (which could be regular expressions) are discussed in detail later in the book. Here, only results with simple patterns are shown.

   sub works for the first occurrence and gsub works for all occurrences in the string (gsub is a *global substitution*).

```
irb(main):007:0> "Hello".sub('H','W')
=> "Wello"
irb(main):008:0> "Hello".sub('l','x')
=> "Hexlo"
irb(main):009:0> "Hello".sub('ll','x')
=> "Hexo"
irb(main):010:0> "Hello".gsub('l','x')
=> "Hexxo"
```

scan

scan has multiple forms. The general (non-block) form returns an array by dividing the string into tokens of the given pattern. It is best understood in the context of regular expressions (discussed in detail in Chapter 7). However, it is a very important string function and hence mentioned here.

   Suppose the pattern /[a-z]+/ means one or more contiguous characters that are anything from a to z. Take a look at the following as an example.

```
irb(main):018:0> "hello world".scan(/[a-z]+/)
=> ["hello", "world"]
```

   It scans in the string for any such pattern (contiguous a–z). Two such patterns are found, and hence the returned array has those two patterns.

Let's look at another example. Suppose /…/ means that a pattern is signified by any three contiguous characters (exactly three). Then, take a look at the following example.

```
irb(main):020:0> "hello world".scan(/.../)
=> ["hel", "lo ", "wor"]
```

It finds only three such patterns because the remaining id is not three characters long.

split

split is a very important function, especially while recognizing columns from an input data file. It splits a string, based on a given separator (or space, if no separator is specified). This is the general form:

```
str.split( pattern=$;, < limit > ) => array
```

A full discussion of the function is not warranted at this point. However, the pattern is optional and could be a regular expression. The limit is also optional (limits, in general, indicate the number of columns that are to be returned; the last column includes the rest of the string).

If limit is omitted, trailing empty fields are suppressed. If it is 1, the entire string is returned as the only element of the array. If it is negative, there is no limit to the number of fields returned; trailing null fields are not suppressed.

The pattern=$! syntax implies that the default value of the pattern is '$;' (which is a predefined variable and the value of that is 'nil' by default. And when occurs, the separator is taken as a single space). Predefined variables are discussed in Chapter 3.

Now it is time for some demonstrations.

```
irb(main):001:0> arr = "hello world".split
=> ["hello", "world"]
irb(main):002:0> arr = "hello world".split(' ')
=> ["hello", "world"]
irb(main):003:0> arr = "hello world".split('  ')
=> ["hello world"]
```

Note, that when two spaces have been given a split pattern, the resulting array has only one element (it could not split on the space in between, because that is a single space).

```
irb(main):004:0> arr = "hello world".split('ll')
=> ["he", "o world"]
irb(main):005:0> arr = "abc,def,ghi".split(',')
=> ["abc", "def", "ghi"]
```

Comma separation is especially useful for CSV file manipulation.

```
irb(main):006:0> arr = "John,Doe,101 Nowhere Street".split(',',2)
=> ["John", "Doe,101 Nowhere Street"]
irb(main):007:0> arr = "John,Doe,101 Nowhere Street   ".split(',',2)
=> ["John", "Doe,101 Nowhere Street   "]
irb(main):009:0> arr = "John,Doe,101 Nowhere Street   ".split(',')
=> ["John", "Doe", "101 Nowhere Street   "]
```

Note how specifying the limit restricts the return array to two elements; the last element has rest of the string.

String Formatting

A string can be formatted in particular ways to print a number in some desired format. The following example briefly illustrates this.

```
puts "zero padding"
x = "%05d" % 123   # should be "00123"
puts x
puts "decimal formatting"
y = "%.2f" % 34.9 # should be "34.90"
puts y
```

2.1 Accepting Input from the Console

Problem

Take input from the console in Ruby.

Solution

If writing to the console uses puts, it is a natural logical extrapolation that the gets function should be used to read from the console.

If you are going to use scripting for batch programming alone, you will possibly never need to read input interactively from console. However, this is a rather basic function of Ruby (and indeed of programming tasks in general) and worth discussing here. Note that this is not the only way you can take input from console, but perhaps this is the most generally programmatic way for Ruby to take input from a console.

Well, a demonstration is in order. Run the following piece of code. Write it in a file and give it a name, such as inp1.rb. Save it and then run it from the console.

```
x = gets
puts x
```

You will find that the execution got stuck at a point (the beginning of the next line to the command) without coming back to the command prompt.

```
=>ruby inp1.rb
```

This is because it is waiting for user input from the console (call to gets).

Provide the number 3 as input and press the Return key. You should observe the following behavior.

```
=>ruby inp1.rb
3
3
```

How It Works

It takes in the value in the x variable and prints it (the value of x) through the puts statement.

Try experimenting with a few other inputs (of different types) and see what happens. (Remember to press the Return key every time after you input).

```
 =>ruby inp1.rb
2.5
2.5
=>ruby inp1.rb
c
c
=>ruby inp1.rb
abc
abc
```

It seems to be handling different types very well on the outset. Note, however, that it is actually taking everything as a string. So the 3 that it printed was a String, not a Fixnum. But even that is not the full story.

Try the following code.

```
x = gets
puts x * 2
```

If you provide 3 as input, it does not produce 6; but you see something that might seem strange at first glance.

```
=>ruby inp2.rb
3
3
3
```

The first 3 is the input given, of course. The other 3s are the output. The occurrence of the string has been multiplied (i.e., essentially two strings added side by side), but notice also that the interpreted value of x has a newline character in it.

2.2 Accepting Numbers as Input

Problem

Accept numbers as input from the console.

Solution

Let's untangle this part by part. First, how to take it as an integer (I would use "integer" instead of Fixnum in many places because somehow it seems more natural).

Let's convert the input using the to_i function.

If you run the following code

```
x = gets.to_i
puts x * 2
```

and provide 3 as input, the result, I would think, is quite as per expectation.

```
=>ruby inpint.rb
3
6
```

How It Works

The to_i function did its job of converting the input to an integer. (Notice the newline is also no longer an issue here.) It would not require a great stretch of imagination to guess that to_f is the corresponding function for converting to Float.

The following code

```
x = gets.to_f
puts x * 2
```

with 2.5 as input, should run as follows.

```
=>ruby inpflt.rb
2.5
5.0
```

2.3 Handling the Newline

Problem

How should the newline be handled for string inputs? For example, how would you accept someone's first name and last name (separately) from the console, in Ruby, and print the full name on a single line?

Solution

As a first approximation, try the following code.

```
puts "First name :"
fname = gets
puts "Last name :"
lname = gets
puts fname + lname
```

Provided that "John" is the first name and "Doe" is the last name, it should go as follows.

```
=>ruby inpstr.rb
First name :
John
Second name :
Doe
John
Doe
```

This is not what was aimed for. The first name and the last name appear on different lines. There should be a way to remove the trailing newlines from the inputs.

The chomp function comes to the rescue. The code changed in the following manner.

```
puts "First name :"
fname = gets.chomp
puts "Last name :"
lname = gets.chomp
puts fname + lname
```

This overcomes the problem.

```
=>ruby inpstr2.rb
First name :
John
Last name :
Doe
JohnDoe
```

The difference, eventually, lies in the chomp function, which trims the newline characters from the (end of the) line read.

Although the outcome is perhaps not ideal because the two parts of the name have no space between them, they do appear on the same line. One way to provide a space is to simply change the last line of the code to this:

```
puts fname + " " + lname
```

Note that the chomp function could have been used on the variables. Check the following code.

```
puts "First name :"
fname = gets
puts "Last name :"
lname = gets
puts fname.chomp + " " + lname.chomp
```

It should run as follows.

```
=>ruby inpstr3.rb
First name :
John
Last name :
Doe
John Doe
```

chomp is very useful for the line-by-line processing of an input data file.

More on Getting Rid of the Newline

I guess that this serious enough to warrant a bit more demonstration.

Consider a programmer writing code in a language that requires each statement to end with a semicolon. He is doing this on a Friday evening with a bottle of beer on his desk. (His office environment is rather relaxed, especially on Friday afternoons. Besides, who would notice? His boss was also drinking.) He needed to finish the piece of code soon; otherwise, he would not have done it while having beer.

After a long while, he noticed that he forgot all the semicolons; although he is pretty sure (that's what he is saying) that everything else is OK and that the code should be otherwise bug free. By this time he already had a good amount of beer in his system. He does not feel like editing the file just to put in so many semicolons at the end of each line, but he needs to compile the code.

Suppose he comes to you for a solution. Perhaps you could do something with a bit of Ruby scripting so that he can quickly compile and test the code, get it done and over with, and head to the nearest pub.

For simplicities' sake, suppose you decide to test his code (to transform it) using only the first four lines.

```
int x = 0
int y = 0
int r = 5
float areavar  = x * x + y * y - r * r
```

This story is fictitious, of course, but now let's look at the actual programming exercise.

■ **Note**   This particular scenario could very easily be done by a regex substitution through a good text editor; but as of now, we will focus on a Ruby solution.

As a first approximation, you may want to try the following code (assume the input file name is coord.txt).

```
infile = File.open('coord.txt','r')
outfile = File.open('modcoord.txt','w')
while (line = infile.gets)
        outfile.puts line + ';'
end
outfile.close
infile.close
```

You will almost be successful—but not quite. The output file has the following content.

```
int x = 0
;
int y = 0
;
int r = 5
;
float areavar  = x * x + y * y - r * r;
```

This is because, except for the last line, each line in the input file comes with a trailing newline character. When the line is read, the character, along with other parts of the line, are added to (assigned as part of) the line variable. When the output string is constructed, the newline part is still there, and hence, the line breaks as they appear.

Change the line containing puts as follows

```
outfile.puts line.chomp  + ';'
```

and then run the program (after saving the file, of course). Now you are truly successful. This is the output:

```
int x = 0;
int y = 0;
int r = 5;
float areavar  = x * x + y * y - r * r;
```

Again, you can see that chomp is a very useful function in Ruby batch programming.

Note that it works equally well when there is a carriage return character along with the new line at the end, and it does not create trouble if there is no newline at the end.

```
irb(main):003:0> str1="abc\n"
=> "abc\n"
irb(main):004:0> str1.chomp
=> "abc"
irb(main):005:0> str2="abc\r\n"
=> "abc\r\n"
irb(main):006:0> str2.chomp
=> "abc"
irb(main):007:0> str3="abc"
=> "abc"
irb(main):008:0> str3.chomp
=> "abc"
```

Note that this function can also take an argument (record separator), although this form is highly unlikely to be used in practice.

```
irb(main):009:0> str="abcd"
=> "abcd"
irb(main):010:0> str.chomp("d")
=> "abc"
```

If nothing is given as an argument (such as in the case study for putting a semicolon at the end), it uses the default, which is a single set of carriage return characters (usually \r\n).

2.4 Formatting Strings

Problem

You need to have a string formatted the way that you want, with one or more variables replaced with their proper values.

This is especially useful for reporting purposes, but also has many other uses. Think of a use case where you have been given a letter format with a subject and text, but the addressee is given as a variable whose values may come from a list people. Essentially, it is the same letter to be sent to multiple people, but addressing each of them separately by name.

Note that in this case (as indeed in many other cases), adding multiple strings with blanks [e.g., + "   " +] is far from the ideal solution).

Solution

Consider the following code.

```
name = "John"
puts "Hello #{name} how are you ?"
```

It should run as follows.

```
=>ruby formstr.rb
Hello John how are you ?
```

How It Works

As you can see, the variable placeholder is defined by variable name encased in #{} within the string (i.e., using a #{<variable name>} construct within the string).

Note that in this case (i.e., for formatted string), the double quotes cannot be replaced by single quotes. In other words, the following code won't work.

```
name = "John"
puts 'Hello #{name} how are you ?'
```

Here, the #{name} part is taken literally, and not as an interpreted value.

```
=>ruby formstr_bad.rb
Hello #{name} how are you ?
```

It is still a valid string, however, and hence no error is thrown.

Does this substitution also work for other basic types of variables, such as Float? What prevents us from experimenting?

Write the following code in a file named formstr2.rb. Save the file and run the code.

```
company = "Rhombus Inc"
year = 2015
total = 1289965.45
puts "In year #{year} net sales of #{company} was #{total} dollars."
```

The result is not disappointing.

```
=>ruby formstr2.rb
In year 2015 net sales of Rhombus Inc was 1289965.45 dollars.
```

Evidently, it also works with integer and float values in the same fashion.

2.5 Processing Command-Line Arguments

Problem

For any serious programming language, being able to accept a command-line argument is probably indispensable. In Java, for instance, the main method has an argument that is an array of strings. These arguments to the main method come from command-line arguments (if any).

Solution

In a Ruby script, a command-line argument is available as a predefined constant (array) named ARGV (note that the name is case sensitive).

Run the following code the usual way.

```
name = ARGV[0]
puts "Hello #{name} how are you ?"
```

The result is not very impressive.

```
=>ruby argvtst.rb
Hello  how are you ?
```

Use a command-line argument, however, and the result is better.

```
=>ruby argvtst.rb John
Hello John how are you ?
```

How It Works

Consider the following:

- It does not wait for the argument (as with C or Java, for instance).

- In Ruby, ARGV[0] denotes the first argument rather than the program name (unlike Java).

- For the Ruby script, it is already available in the context. Even though we did not have any explicitly defined main method with named parameter(s), predefined constants can be used this way.

- An array is a type of collection that you are most likely familiar with from another programming language. Clearly, in Ruby arrays are zero-based (the index starts with 0) and the elements are accessed as <Array-name>[<index_number>]. (e.g., ARGV[0]).

In order to accept a second argument, you would use ARGV[1].
Try the following code. You shouldn't be disappointed.

```
first_name = ARGV[0]
last_name = ARGV[1]
puts "Hello #{first_name} #{last_name} how are you ?"
```

It should run as follows.

```
=>ruby argvtst2.rb John Doe
Hello John Doe how are you ?
```

It is easy to extrapolate what you could do to work with three arguments.

2.6 Reading from a File

Problem

One of the very basic tasks that you may need to perform for a lot of scripting
functionalities is reading data from a file. Quite often you need to read part of a file based
on certain criteria—for example, a column containing pieces of data with particular
values (e.g., a person's address). So, you need to know some basic operations, such as
opening a file in read mode.

Solution

In the chapter code directory, create a file named input.txt with only one line of text
that contains the word welcome.
    In the same directory, you need a readfl.rb program file with the following content.

```
infile = File.open('input.txt','r')
myword = infile.gets
puts myword
infile.close
```

Run the code from the command prompt. It should look like this:

```
=>ruby readfl.rb
welcome
```

How It Works

A bit of explanation is in order.

The first line of code, `infile = File.open('input.txt','r')`, means this:

1. Open a file (from current directory) named `input.txt`.

2. In read mode.

3. And store the file handler in a variable named `infile`.

The `infile` file handler is needed for further operations on the file.

In order to read a line, the `gets` function is used; however, this time it is called on the (`infile.gets`) file handler, hence the instruction is to read the input from the file, which is then stored in the variable named `myword`.

The third line (`puts myword`) is for output of the value of `myword`. Note that it is not using the #{} construct, as it is not within a string any longer, being output by itself without any other string concatenated.

The fourth line simply closes the file (which was opened for reading) by calling the `close` function on the handler.

The second and third lines could have been combined in a single line, as follows.

```
puts infile.gets
```

The same effect would have been achieved. But for the purpose of better understanding and clarity, the first form is preferable. (Consider someone else trying to maintain your code).

Further down the road (figuratively speaking), there are recipes that focus on more interesting issues related to reading from a file.

2.7 Writing to a File

Problem

How do you write to a file in Ruby?

Solution

Try the following code.

```
outfile = File.open('output.txt','w')
myword = 'welcome'
outfile.puts myword
outfile.close
```

You should not be surprised if it works. The command prompt should reappear (after running the program) and you should find a file named output.txt created with two lines. The first line has the word welcome (following a newline character, which causes the second line).

How It Works

For opening the file (the first line of code), the file name was given. The mode in this case is w (open for writing).

If you are to perform a write operation on a file, it cannot be opened in read mode. There are other modes possible, however (such as a for append mode, and r+ for "read and"—as in "read and write"). One of the valid modes can be chosen based on the use case. (However, at this point, let's make do with the w mode).

The puts function has been called on the output file handler to output the value of the myword variable. This line (outfile.puts myword) does the writing. The last line closes the file.

If you run the code repeatedly, you will find that the file is getting overwritten (the modification timestamp should update).

But how does the program behave if you are trying to read an input file that is not present?

Rename the file input.txt to input1.txt and run the readfl.rb program written earlier. It comes back with an error.

```
=>ruby readfl.rb
readfl.rb:1:in `initialize': No such file or directory @ rb_sysopen -
input.txt (Errno::ENOENT)
        from readfl.rb:1:in `open'
        from readfl.rb:1:in `<main>'
```

This doesn't look very nice, does it?

The situation is understandable, as the file does not exist. In a situation like this, it may be more desirable (especially for the end user of the batch code, who may be a non-IT person or may not have a programming background) to trap the error and provide a more user-friendly message. (Remember, sometimes a set of error messages is more voluminous and it may be difficult even for the developer to quickly get to the real cause of the error). Recipe 2.8 deals with this.

2.8 Getting Started with Exception Handling

Problem

How do you provide a user-friendly user message when the file to be read is not present? (Note that exceptions refer to runtime issues, not syntax errors).

Solution

Try the following code.

```
begin
        infile = File.open('input.txt','r')
        myword = infile.gets
        puts myword
        infile.close
rescue
        puts "Could not find file input.txt"
end
```

It should look like this:

```
=>ruby tstexcp.rb
Could not find file input.txt
```

Although the file is not found, the message is much more user-friendly.

Initial Execution Context

Prior to the previous code, all the programs (except for loop) contained a set of instructions (statements) one after another. There was no resemblance to an explicit block structure; however, the last program does resemble a block structure. Why is that? A bit of explanation about the initial context of a Ruby program will help.

If you are familiar with C and Java, you may know that the entry point for a stand-alone application in those languages is usually the main function. However, a Ruby program seems to work right from the go. So where is the entry point?

The initial execution context for a usual Ruby program is an implicit object called main (not the method but an object). Here "object" has the same meaning as an instance of a class in object-oriented programming. It is an instance of the Object class (but this is not the right place to thoroughly discuss classes and objects in Ruby.) Any plain statement that you add to a Ruby script implicitly is added to this object. Not only that, it is added to an implicit block (with both begin and end implicit).

So when you write this:

```
puts "Hello"
```

In effect, it is this:

```
begin
puts "Hello"
end
```

Execution starts from the first statement of this block.

■ **Tip**   If it helps, you may think about a series of plain statements in a Ruby script (such as most of the code so far in this book) as statements written in the `main` method in a Java program. (Although in terms of pure technicality, this is not an exact analogy, but it may help with you initial understanding).

A little experiment may help you understand the initial execution context. Type the following code in a file named `tstmain.rb`.

```
puts1 "Hello"
```

Note that the wrong function name is intentional. Save and close the file and try to run it. It should throw a syntax error. (What is interesting is the content of the error message).

```
=>ruby tstmain.rb
tstmain.rb:1:in `<main>': undefined method `puts1' for main:Object
(NoMethodError)
Did you mean?  puts
               putc
```

Note that in the error message, the `puts1` method is being pointed to as part of the `main:Object` (an object named `main` of the `Object` type/class). That (the `main` object) is the initial execution context here.

The `begin` and `end`, however, had to be put explicitly in the code in discussion (for reading from a file with exception handling) in order to use the `rescue` construct.

The `begin-rescue-end` construct in Ruby works somewhat like the `try-catch` construct in Java (again, not an exact analogy). One block may have multiple rescues. One untagged rescue (just `rescue`) works like a catch-all type exception handler (like `Exception` in Java, as opposed to say `FileNotFoundException`). An error can be raised explicitly, but in this case, an explicit one was not needed. The file was designed not to be found (to get the error).

This is a rather brief discussion on exception handling. But for now, this is all you need (and perhaps more). This book, being what it is, does not make you an expert. But it also does not require you to spend as much time as you would if you were to become an expert.

2.9 Importing Code

Problem

Quite often, a software program is developed as a project involving multiple files. As a whole, the code may solve a single problem or (more commonly) address multiple aspects of the solution as a whole. For such programs, importing external classes, constants, and so forth, is often a necessity because (for instance) a function defined in a class (in another file) may be needed to be called from the current program (program defined in the current file). But even otherwise, it may be necessary to include reference to external code, which is part of the standard language library (but not necessarily loaded by default) or while using a third-party library.

How do you include or import code written in another file in Ruby?

Solution

Java does it through import. C has include, for instance. They are somewhat equivalent to require in Ruby.

■ **Note**   require works at the file level; that is, when using require, you include the contents of a file, not a class or package. The content may very well be a class definition, but you are essentially including the content code, which happens to be defining a class.

Creating and deleting directories, for instance, requires the FileUtils module. But when the program specifies require 'fileutils', it is in fact including the contents of the fileutils.rb file, which should be available in the standard path for Ruby program loading (if the installation is correct) and happens to be defining the FileUtils module. This standard path is known as $LOAD_PATH (a predefined variable for Ruby programming environment).

A module in Ruby is a way of grouping methods, classes, and constants together. If you are familiar with Java, think of a package (although that is somewhat crude equivalence).

The require in a require statement is actually a call to a method named require. The require method is used to load another file and execute all of its statements. This serves to import all class and method definitions in the file.

2.10 Creating and Deleting Directories

Problem

Working with directories may be needed for many day-to-day tasks. For example, consider that you have been given a directory that includes a lot of files with different extensions. Some of them have sql extensions, which are code files; others have dat extensions, which are data files. You may want to separate those files, based on their extensions, into two different directories. Working with directories in such fashion is perhaps not done as often as reading from or writing to files, but it is still very useful knowledge.

Solution

Run the following code.

```
require 'fileutils'
FileUtils.mkdir('credit')
```

A directory named credit is created under the current directory (unless it exists already, of course).

Deleting isn't hugely different. Replacing the mkdir_p function with the rm_rf function should do the trick.

```
require 'fileutils'
FileUtils.rm_rf('credit')
```

■ **Note**   There is no complaint with deleting if the directory does not exist. This is the same behavior when creating a directory. So if your program is working with the expectation that the directory should always exist prior to deletion, you may want to put checks in place to ensure that it is.

How It Works

mkdir is a method defined in the FileUtils module (which can be accessed as FileUtils.mkdir). If you do not load the fileutils.rb file (i.e., if you omitted the require statement), FileUtils is unknown to the program—and running it would produce an error.

A module is a way of grouping together methods, classes, and constants. (Although that is not all a module is about). If you were to define some methods that are not instance-specific (like static methods), a module may be a good place to define them. In Java, in a similar situation, you might have used a package, but the analogy is rather remote.

2.11 Creating a Whole Directory Path

Problem

How do you create an entire directory path (e.g., a/b/c) in Ruby?

Solution

A slightly different variation of file creation using the mkdir is mkdir_p function, which creates all directories in the path as required.

How It Works

Try the following code to see the effect.

```
require 'fileutils'
FileUtils.mkdir_p('region/div/dept')
```

Alternatively, for the same directory structure (i.e., multiple directories with the '/' separator), if you used mkdir instead of mkdir_p, things would not be so smooth. The following code produces an error.

```
require 'fileutils'
FileUtils.mkdir('region/div/dept')
```

For a better error message, for this case too, you can use rescue.

```
begin
        require 'fileutils'
        FileUtils.mkdir('region/div/dept')
rescue
        puts 'Wrong function used'
end
```

Although that does not solve the problem of functionality, it does present the case nicely.

```
=>ruby crpath1.rb
Wrong function used
```

2.12 Reading Multiple Lines from a File

Problem

What if you need to read multiple lines instead of one from an input line?

The following is the earlier program.

```
infile = File.open('input.txt','r')
myword = infile.gets
puts myword
infile.close
```

If you were to use it on a three-line input file, as follows, it would output the first line only.

```
welcome
to
Seattle
```

However, in a batch script, quite often you may need to scan through all the lines in an input file. In contrast, this program opens the file, reads only the first line, prints it out on the console, and closes the file.

35

Solution

Between opening and closing the files, the middle part (reading and printing out) needs to be done until the input file has exhausted all lines.

A while loop can be used to do the job nicely. Although this is not the only possible way, it can be considered a general enough approach.

```ruby
infile = File.open('inplines.txt','r')
while (line = infile.gets)
        puts line
end
infile.close
```

■ **Note** Prior to running the code, create a multiline text file in the directory named inplines.txt.

The code should run as expected and print all three lines.

```
=>ruby readmulti.rb
welcome
to
Seattle
```

How It Works

Ruby offers some control statements. (You would have already seen for). while is one such control statement. This is the normal construct of a while statement:

```ruby
while (condition)
                statements
end
```

Here, the while (condition) line serves as the beginning of the block and the end marks the end of the block.

The condition is expected to evaluate to a Boolean (true or false). Hence, this code

```ruby
a = 0
while (a < 5)
        a = a + 1
        puts a
end
```

produces the following output (note that there would be a blank line after 5, as puts adds a new line at the end of the output string).

1
2
3
4
5

That was a bit of general discussion on while. Let's come back to the code for reading lines from the file. Note that this is the while line:

```
while (line = infile.gets)
```

This means that the following condition is as follows.

```
line = infile.gets
```

But wasn't it supposed to be a Boolean? Yet this is an assignment, isn't it?

It is actually both an assignment and a Boolean. This is one of the peculiarities of Ruby, if you are coming from a Java background, for instance.

First, for any assignment in Ruby, after the right-hand side expression is evaluated, the value that is assigned to the variable is the value of the whole assignment (i.e., the assignment itself evaluated to that value).

■ **Note** The same applies to return values of function calls in Ruby. (i.e., the function itself evaluates to that value).

Hence, the value of the statement a = 2 + 3 + 5 is 10, which is the value posted to the a variable after the expression evaluation. So the a variable and the assignment as a whole both evaluate to 10 in this case.

Second, the gets function (used on the infile object) returns nil if it fails to read a line. nil in Ruby is equivalent to null (as in Java). And nil is treated as false in a Boolean context (for instance, if you assign nil to a condition that expects a Boolean, the nil will be taken as false).

Hence, when no more lines are found (all the lines have been read), infile.gets returns nil, which is the value of the assignment at that point, which in this case means false, and the while loop breaks free. So long as the lines are available (unless there are any other errors that prevent reading), they are assigned in turn to the line variable (for a proper line, the assignment would evaluate to true and the while will go on).

The line variable may be used inside the loop body for processing purposes. The choice of the name of the variable representing a line (line in this case) is arbitrary.

This construct with while (line = infile.gets) is a convenient way to read an input file, line by line, and process the data therein.

Things can get slightly better (definitely from a typing point of view) with while. Remember the part about function arguments not requiring parentheses? This makes puts "Hello" and puts("Hello") equivalent. Hence, this statement

```
infile = File.open('inplines.txt','r')
```

can be replaced with the following one.

```
infile = File.open 'inplines.txt','r'
```

(Don't miss the gap between the end of open and the beginning of input.txt.)

Well, it happens with conditions too. Hence, you can safely omit the parentheses and write the while line (line containing while and condition) as follows.

```
while line = infile.gets
```

Our earlier code for a multiline read may boil down to this:

```
infile = File.open 'inplines.txt','r'
while line = infile.gets
        puts line
end
infile.close
```

It still works as usual. In fact, if you need only one statement inside the while (like here), you can make the entire while loop inline instead of the while block, and it still works.

```
puts line while line = infile.gets
```

The code is now three lines in total.

```
infile = File.open 'inplines.txt','r'
puts line while line = infile.gets
infile.close
```

2.13 Reading a File in One Shot

Problem

You need to read the whole file in one shot (i.e., in a single string).

Solution

Use the read function on the file as follows, for example.

```
text = File.read 'inplines.txt'
puts text
```

It should run as follows, printing all the lines (which are part of the text string variable in this program).

```
=>ruby fullfl.rb
welcome
to
Seattle
```

How It Works

First, be aware that for a rather big file, this may not be a good idea. Reading the entire file directly into memory can stop a machine in its tracks if the file is too big. It should be done only when you know in advance how big the file is and you've got plenty of RAM.

Second, note that the code is not using any file handler (so the file need not be explicitly closed from the program).

Third, the newlines are part of the string. (This has to be catered for if you want to extract individual lines from the text string for processing).

One use case (but not the only one by any means), could be when you are looking for multiple occurrences of a particular word in a file, but the word may be split across lines (without a hyphen or space at the split point, just the newline).

2.14 Working with Strings

Problem

You want to work with strings in Ruby.

Solution

If you know any other programming language, chances are that you already understand strings.

Strings in Ruby are a sequence of characters (or bytes) that are typically used to represent text. Strings are objects of the String class in Ruby.

How It Works

There are many ways to construct a string literal, all of which are not equally used (and hence, probably not worth thinking much about unless you want to learn the language comprehensively). In my opinion, the following are the more prominent ones.

- Encased in single quotes:

```
'This is a book'
'That isn\'t the case' => That isn't the case
'double quote " n' => double quote " n
```

■ **Note**   In this form, you cannot use a variable substitution using #{expression}.

- Encased in double quotes:

```
"Hello World"
"isn't it"  => isn't it
"The value is #{2 +3}" => The value is 5
```

You would have already seen that the expression in #{expression} can be a variable (e.g., #{name}). However, this can even be one or more statements. The following code

```
puts "Check this out #{
            j = 0
            for i in 1..5
              j = j + i
            end
            j}"
```

translates as follows.

```
Check this out 15
```

Being a sequence of characters, certain characters in a string can be accessed using index (in this sense, it behaves like an array [a zero-based array]). Hence, the following code prints e (the second character) followed by a newline.

```
a = "Hello"
puts a[1]
```

Concatenation

You have already seen a string concatenation with the + operator.

```
'abc' + 'def' => "abcdef"
```

Expression Evaluation

String expression evaluation can also be used to concatenate strings.

Note, you cannot straightaway add an integer to a string. "Hello" + 3 will result in an error (although this is permitted in Java).

```
irb(main):001:0> "Hello" + 3
TypeError: no implicit conversion of Fixnum into String
        from (irb):1:in `+'
        from (irb):1
```

This is the way forward:

```
irb(main):002:0> "Hello #{3}"
=> "Hello 3"
```

There are other ways of concatenating an integer or float to a string.

2.15 Converting Numbers to a String

Problem

How do you convert an integer or a float to a string, and vice versa?

Solution

When called on a string, the to_i function makes it an integer (Fixnum). This is especially useful for reading from a console or an input file, (when the data is expected to be an integer). Note that it does not complain when the data is not integer. For a string (not a number), it simply returns 0. (So you need to be careful; otherwise, for the wrong data, it might silently produce result that may be far from what you expected, and not easy to recognize as wrong.)

```
irb(main):001:0> "12".to_i
=> 12
irb(main):002:0> "12.5".to_i
=> 12
irb(main):003:0> "abc".to_i
=> 0
```

The to_f function is similar except, it converts to a float.

```
"12".to_f => 12.0
"12.5".to_f => 12.5
"abc".to_f => 0.0
```

The to_s function (although available on a string also) is more useful when called on other things, especially an integer (Fixnum) or a float (Float).

Notice that "Hello" + 3 causes an error, but the following works perfectly.

```
irb(main):006:0> "Hello " + 3.to_s
=> "Hello 3"
```

The to_i and to_f functions have been discussed already in the context of reading input from a console (see Recipe 2.1). Here they were presented briefly for the sake of putting them in one place.

2.16 Extracting Information from Strings

Problem

A string, such as a line from a file, may contain information, only part of which may be of interest in a certain context. For instance, a data file may contain the first name, last name, age, and telephone number of people (let's say customers), one record per line. If you wish to know the name of the youngest person in the data available in the file, the name and age is important, but the telephone number has no relevance.

Thus, it is often useful to be able to extract information contained as part of a string, and then work on this information. How do you go about doing that?

This section describes a couple of tasks and demonstrates in context.

Task: Change the Order of Names

A data file named nameaddr.csv consists of three columns: last name, first name, and first line of the address.

```
carver,anita,12 Ross St
dell,sarah,15 Jesse St
yehuda,perez,20 Margaret St
chinoy,ron,23 Madox Square
```

The task is to print (modified) records in a file so that the resulting record only has the <first name> and the <last name> separated by a space and both capitalized. The following illustrates an example.

```
carver,anita,12 Ross St => Anita Carver
```

Solution

The following code should do the trick.

```
infile = File.open('nameaddr.csv','r')
outfile = File.open('names.txt','w')
while (line = infile.gets)
        arr = line.chomp.split(',')
        outfile.puts arr[1].capitalize + " " + arr[0].capitalize
end
outfile.close
infile.close
```

How It Works

This code uses the chomp, split, and capitalize functions, as well as concatenating using +.

Task: Totaling the Shopping List

Given the following content in an input file (like the prices of items from shopping), write a program to calculate the total amount spent. It is a CSV file named shopping. csv. The format is item_name, quantity (the number of units or another measure; for example, 1 implies 1 unit, or 1kg, or 1 liter, based on the unit specified), unit_price, and a description of unit, separated by a single space.

```
Banana,6,2.50 each
Eggplant,2,10.00 per kg
Milk,3,4.50 per litre
Cold drinks,6,8.25 per bottle
```

Solution

Clearly, the result should be the sum of each of first set of numbers multiplied by each of second set of numbers. However, note that just separating by a comma won't give you the second set of numbers.

The following code should work.

```
infile = File.open('shopping.csv','r')
sum = 0
while (line = infile.gets)
        arr = line.chomp.split(',')
        arr2 = arr[2].split(' ')
        sum = sum + arr[1].to_i * arr2[0].to_f
end
infile.close
puts sum
```

(If the result is not as expected, in the input file, check if the unit price and unit description have more than one space in between them in any line).

Exercises

The solutions to these exercises are in the appendix.

Exercise 2.1

Given a text file with multiple lines, write a program to print the line with the maximum number of characters and the number of characters that it has. Assume that the input file has a distinct maximum (i.e., only one line has the maximum number of characters).

Exercise 2.2

A palindrome is a sentence (case and spaces ignored) reads exactly the same back to front. This is an example (a crude one): *You are erauoy*. This is a better example: *A man, a plan, a canal—Panama*. For now, however, use inputs that do not have punctuation marks.

Write a program to find out if a given string is a palindrome. (Read lines from a file and determine if each of them are a palindrome or not).

CHAPTER 3

■ ■ ■

Language Elements

This chapter takes a slightly different approach and discusses some elements of the language. This provides some foundation for you to work on later recipes. Perhaps comments are a good starting point.

Commenting on Commenting

Ruby programs have two types of comments:

- A # and anything that follows until the end of the line (unless the # is used in a string and escaped appropriately) makes an in line or single line comment. For example,

```
print "abcd" #this is a comment
```

- A block comment may be written as shown in the following program between =begin and =end lines.

```
print "abcd"
=begin
everything between the line above
and the line below is a comment
=end
```

In this case, the equal signs (=) must be the first characters of the respective lines. No space is allowed after the equal signs.

Variables, Operators …

Ruby has basic types, such as numbers and strings. It supports Boolean expressions. It also has ranges that may come handy. Let's start with numbers.

© Malay Mandal 2016
M. Mandal, *Ruby Recipes*, DOI 10.1007/978-1-4842-2469-4_3

Working with Numbers

Ruby supports integer and floating-point numbers. Integers can be of any length (the limit is determined by the amount of free memory on your system). Integers within a certain range (say, between –2 to the power 30 *and* 2 to the power 30 – 1) are held internally in binary form and are objects of the Fixnum class. Larger integers are object of the Bignum class. The back-and-forth conversion is internally handled by Ruby.

A number with a decimal point and/or an exponent is turned into a Float object. *The decimal point must be both preceded and followed by (one or more) digit(s) when you are supplying a float literal*; otherwise, the decimal point will be misinterpreted because the dot (.) is a way to invoke a method on an object.

Table 3-1 provides some basic arithmetic operations available on all of those types of numbers (Fixnum, Bignum, and Float).

Table 3-1. Basic Arithmetic Operations

Operation	Symbol	Example
addition	+	5 + 2 => 7 5 + 2.0 => 7.0
subtraction	-	5 - 2 => 3
multiplication	*	5 * 2 => 10
division	/	5 / 2 => 2 5/2.0 => 2.5
modulo	%	5 % 2 => 1
exponentiation	**	5 ** 2 => 25

Note 5 / 2 in the table. Since both are integers, the result is an integer that leaves out the decimal. But when one of them is Float object, it is lifted to float.

The non-declaration of variables has already been discussed.

In general, the evaluation of an expression and assignment occurs similarly to many other languages. Operator precedence and the role of parentheses in basic arithmetic operation are similar too.

```
(3 + 6) / (2 + 1) => 3
3 + 6 / 2 + 1 => 7
```

In Ruby, variables are objects of some class or the other. To see which class is a variable's type, you can call the print method on it and print the result.

This next code

```
a = 3
b = 2.5
print a.class
print b.class
```

runs as follows.

```
=>ruby chktyp.rb
FixnumFloat=>
```

Notice that the command prompt appears immediately and two outputs are printed on the same line. This is because the print function, unlike puts, does not add a newline character at the end of the string automatically; otherwise, they work in a similar fashion.

The fact that normal variables are objects of classes makes it possible to call methods on them using the dot notation (and sometimes without the dot notation). Because of this, the following code

```
a = 2
b = 2.
c = a + b
print c
```

ends in an error (in line 3).

```
test.rb:3:in `+': nil can't be coerced into Fixnum (TypeError)
        from test.rb:3:in `<main>'
```

■ **Note**   Ruby interprets semicolons and newlines as end of statements, unless the line ends with an operator or a backslash.

The value of b ended in a dot (.). It has possibly been interpreted that somebody wanted to call a function on 2 and assign the result to b; however, the call did not happen. So b is a nil object in this case and hence the + operation fails.

Make sure to precede and follow a decimal point with at least one digit (on either side) when you supply a float literal.

A few other function calls on numbers are shown in Table 3-2.

Table 3-2. *Function Calls on Numbers*

Function	Description	Example
abs	Absolute value	-3.abs => 3 3.abs => 3
div	Division	10.div(2) => 5
zero?	Is it zero (returns boolean value)	10.zero? => false
ceil	Ceiling	2.6.ceil => 3
floor	Floor	2.6.floor => 2
round	Round to specified decimal	2.635.round(2) => 2.64

Logical and Other Operators

It is not easy (if at all possible) to provide examples of operator usage without variables, and in order to exemplify variables in action, the same goes for the role of operators. I will discuss some more operators before going into other types of variables.

Arithmetic operators have already been discussed in some detail.

There are some comparison operators, such as those shown in Table 3-3.

Table 3-3. *Comparison Operators*

Operators	Description	Example
==	Equal (check for equality)	3 == 3 => true 6 == 3 => false
!=	Not equal (opposite of equality check)	3 != 3 => false
>	Greater than	4 > 3 => true
<	Less than	4 < 3 => false
>=	Greater than or equal to	4 >= 3 => true 4 >= 4 => true
<=	Less than or equal to	4 <= 3 => false 4 <= 5 => true

In addition, === is used to test equality in a when clause of a case statement.

Reference and Value Equality

- .eql? – Equality (True if the receiver and argument have the same type and equal value)

- .equal? – Equality (True if the receiver and argument have the same object id)

Thus, the following prints true for eql? and false for equal?.

```
a = "ed"
b = "ed"
puts a.eql?(b)
puts a.equal?(b)
```

Checking If an Object Is nil

The nil? method can be used on any object.

```
irb(main):001:0> a = [1] # an array of 1 element
=> [1]
irb(main):002:0> a[1].nil? #a[1] refers to secondelement of the array, which
does not exist
```

```
=> true
irb(main):003:0> a[0].nil?
=> false
```

General Comparison Operator

<=> is the general comparison operator (returns –1, 0, or +1 based on whether its receiver is less than, equal to, or greater than its argument). It is very handy in sorting strings.

Here are some examples of comparison.

```
irb(main):001:0> 3.<=>5
=> -1
irb(main):002:0> 5.<=>3
=> 1
irb(main):003:0> "abc".<=>"def"
=> -1
irb(main):004:0> "abcd".<=>"abc"
=> 1
irb(main):005:0> "abc".<=>"abc"
=> 0
```

Assignment Operators

There are assignment operators, such as the following:

```
= , += , -=, *=, /=, %=, **=
```

Amongst these, = is a pure assignment to a variable. For example, the following assigns 3 to the a variable.

```
a = 3
```

But for others (e.g., +=) it is a mix of an assignment and a binary operation, of which the left operand is the variable assigned (but the prior value of the variable). For example,

```
a += 3
```

is equivalent to

```
a = a + 3
```

The right-hand side a is the prior value of a (prior to the addition), which is added to 3 and assigned back to a again (effectively increasing the value of a by 3). Similarly, the following effectively multiplies the value in a by 3.

```
a *= 3 #equivalent to a = a * 3
```

Mass Assignment

It is worth noting that you can assign values to multiple variables in one go. For instance, the following code assigns the value 1 to the variable a, the value 2 to b and so on.

```
a,b,c,d = 1,2,3,4
```

The types, as usual, need not be the same. The following is valid.

```
a,b,c = 1, 'hello', 2
```

When the count does not match, the extra values (if any) are ignored silently.

```
a,b,c = 1,2,3,4 #4 is ignored
```

And when the variable is extra, the variables toward the end, which do not have any corresponding value, are not assigned (the value is nil).

```
a,b,c,d = 1,2,3 #d will be nil
```

Bitwise, Logical, and Ternary Operators

The following are bitwise operators:

- & (binary AND)
- | (binary OR)
- ^ (binary XOR)
- ~ (binary ones complement)
- << (binary left-shift)
- >> (binary right-shift)

They operate at the bit level. (There is no further use of them in this book, however, and they are rarely used in normal programming tasks).

The following are logical operators:

- and (logical and)
- or (logical or)
- not (logical not)
- && (logical and)
- || (logical or)
- ! (logical not)

Their usage is very reasonable, even from a normal logical argument point of view. For instance, something that is "red and sweet" means that it is both red and sweet (i.e., red is true for it and sweet or sweetness is true for it).

Similarly, the logical operator and (small case) binds two logical arguments, and returns true only if both arguments are true. Thus,

```
irb(main):010:0> (4 > 3) and (4 < 5)
=> true
irb(main):012:0> (4 > 3) and (3 > 5)
=> false
```

Logical or, on the other hand, is satisfied if at least one of the contributing logical arguments is true.

```
irb(main):013:0> (4 > 3) or (3 > 5)
=> true
```

The ternary operator (? :)of the form condition?expression1:expression 2 (a space on either side of ? and : is optional) implies that if the condition evaluates to true, the value is expression 1; otherwise, the value is expression 2. It can be used very effectively in assignments. The following is an example.

```
irb(main):001:0> x = 3
=> 3
irb(main):002:0> y = (x > 0) ? "positive" : "non-positive"
=> "positive"
irb(main):003:0> puts y
positive
=> nil
```

The Range Operators

The following are range operators (range is discussed later):

- • ... - Creates a range with the specified start and end points included (e.g., 1..5 means create a range from 1 to 5)

- • ... - Creates a range with the specified start point included, but the end point is excluded (e.g., 1...5 means create a range from 1 to 4)

The dot (.) Operator

The dot (.) operator is one of the most widely used operators in Ruby. It is used to call the method of a module or a class, such as -3.abs.

51

Some Other Operators

The defined? operator is a special operator that takes the form of a method call to determine whether the expression passed to it is defined. It returns a description string of the expression that is defined, but is nil otherwise. This (the defined? operator) can be used in many ways.

```
irb(main):008:0> a = 1
=> 1
irb(main):009:0> defined? a
=> "local-variable"
irb(main):010:0> defined? b
=> nil
irb(main):011:0> defined? 3
=> "expression"
...
```

The :: (colon) operator is used to access constants, instance methods, and class methods accessed outside of the class or module in which it is defined.

Pattern Matching Operators

The pattern matching operators (especially =~) are very useful for text parsing. Both of these operators work with a string and a regular expression pattern.

- =~ has a match (the string contains at least one match for the regular expression). Returns the position (of the first match) if it does, otherwise returns *nil*.

- !~ has no match.

These operators are best described in the context of regular expressions, but here are some simple examples.

```
irb(main):015:0> "hello" =~ /el/
=> 1
irb(main):016:0> "hello" =~ /xx/
=> nil
irb(main):017:0> "hello" !~ /lo/
=> false
```

Using Ranges

Ranges such as 0 to 9, 'a' to 'z', and so on, are supported in Ruby. A range is created with .. or ... operators. The ... operator excludes the specified end point; for example, 1..5 indicates a range 1 to 5 and 1...5 indicates a range 1 to 4.

Internally, ranges are not represented as list, but as a Range object containing reference to two other objects. For instance, a range of 1..100 is held as a Range object containing reference to two Fixnum objects.

A range can be used in Ruby as intervals, sequences, or conditions.

Interval

A range can be used for an interval test (whether a value falls within the interval or not) by using the case equality operator (===). It returns true or false based on whether the range falls within the interval.

The following code

```
print (1..9)===5
```

prints

```
true
```

and the following code

```
print (1...5)===5
```

prints

```
false
```

Sequences

Ranges can be used as a sequence of values. And being objects, a range used as such is open to the that method calls on them.

```
a = 1..5
print a
```

prints

```
1..5
```

and so does

```
print 1..5
```

However, a range is very handy if you want to initialize an array.
This code

```
arr = (1..5).to_a
print arr
```

53

prints as follows.

```
[1, 2, 3, 4, 5]
```

This code

```
arr = ('a'..'e').to_a
print arr
```

prints as follows.

```
["a", "b", "c", "d", "e"]
```

And the following code

```
arr = ('car'..'cat').to_a
print arr
```

prints as follows.

```
["car", "cas", "cat"]
```

Ranges implement methods. Based on their suitability, many different functionalities can be achieved using those methods.

The following code illustrates some of them.

```
digits = 0..9
print digits.min
puts
print digits.max
puts
print digits.include?(5)
        It prints
0
9
true
```

Conditions

Ranges can be used as conditional expressions in various control flow structures. The following code illustrates usage with a case statement.

```
marks = 65
remark = case marks
        when 0..49 then "below average"
        when 51..100 then "above average"
```

```
        else "average"
end
print remark
```

This is the output.

```
above average
```

Conditional Constructs/Control Flow

Ruby has many control flow statements. Some of them have more than one form syntax-wise. Overall, when used properly, they can sometimes give rise to a rather English-language-like lucid reading of the code
(to an extent).

if

if is the general form.

```
if condition
    code
elsif condition
    code
else
    code
end
```

if, elsif, else, and end are keywords. The following code is an example.

```
a = 0;
if a == 0
      print "zero"
elsif a > 0
      print "positive"
else
      print "negative"
end
```

There may be zero, one, or more elsif keywords. With no elsif or else, (i.e., only the if) and there is a single statement in the code block, the if followed by the condition can come after the statement, in-line, and the end keyword is not needed. So, this

```
a = 1
print "positive" if a > 0
```

is equivalent to the following.

```
a = 1
if a > 0
print "positive"
end
```

If you want to put the statement (of the if body) after the condition and in the same line, use the then keyword (as shown in the following code).

```
a = 5
if a > 0 then print "positive" end
```

Multiple conditions can be combined logically to form a single condition (using and, &&, or, and so on).

For example, this

```
a = 5
if a > 0 and a < 10
        print "positive single digit"
end
```

prints this:

```
positive single digit
```

Keep in mind that nil is interpreted as false in a conditional context. (For a combined condition, the returned value may be nil or anything else, instead of true or false, and nil is interpreted as false).

The following code

```
b = "abc" =~ /c/
c = true
print b && c
```

prints as follows.

```
true
```

(In this case, both b and c are true) and the following code prints nothing.

```
b = "abc" =~ /d/
c = true
print b && c
```

But b && c returns nil. (It will be clearer in irb).

```
irb(main):066:0> b = "abc" =~ /d/
=> nil
irb(main):067:0> c = true
=> true
irb(main):068:0> print b && c
=> nil
```

nil check

You can use .nil? to check whether an object is nil.

The following code illustrates this.

```
b = "abc" =~ /d/
c = true
d = b && c
print d.nil?
```

It prints as follows.

```
true
```

This may come handy in many situations (e.g., checking if something is null, etc.).

Coming back to nil and conditions, the following code

```
b = "abc" =~ /d/
c = "abc" =~ /c/
print "b true" if b
print "c true" if c
```

prints as follows.

```
c true
```

b is nil in the context of the condition, so it is treated as false.

Statements in Ruby return the last expression evaluated. So true && 5 returns 5. Not being nil, 5 is interpreted as true in a conditional context (the value is not converted to true but left as 5).

The following code illustrates this.

```
a = true
b = 5
puts a && b
print  "working" if a && b
```

And it prints as shown in the following.

```
5
working
```

unless

Certain syntaxes in Ruby make it somewhat English-like. If you think about the if modifier, you may find the bias (if I can call it bias). "Do the cooking if not tired" is more natural (English-like) compared to "If not tired do the cooking end."

unless in Ruby is in some way similar to if, but a counterpart (meaning "if not" in English). And this too may as well be another attempt (in case there was any such conscious drive to make it English-like) at making Ruby more like English.

An example is given in the following code.

```
a = -5
unless a >= 0
        print "negative"
else
        print "positive or zero"
end
```

Anything that you can accomplish with unless, you should also be able to do with if.

Ternary operator

The ternary operator can act as a conditional (if-else) and is very handy in conditional assignment.

This is an example.

```
marks = 36
result = marks >= 40 ? 'pass' : 'fail'
print result
prints 'fail'
```

case

Ruby supports case statements (which are somewhat like multiple if-elsif-else statements).

It comes in two forms, as shown next.

```
#Form 1
#plain case (more like if-elsif-else)
[variable = ] case
```

```
when bool_condition
        statements
when bool_condition
        statements
else # the else clause is optional
        statements
end

#Form 2
# Case on an expression:
[variable = ] case expression
when nil
        statements #execute if the expr was nil
when Type1 [ , Type2 ] # e.g., Symbol, String
        statements #execute if the expr
        #resulted in Type1 or Type2 etc.
when value1 [ , value2 ]
        statements #execute if the expr
        #equals value1 or value2 etc.
when /regexp1/ [ , /regexp2/ ]
statements #execute if the expr
        #matches regexp1 or regexp 2 etc.
when min1..max1 [ , min2..max2 ] #i.e., range(s)
        statements #execute if the expr is in the range
        #from min1 to max1 or min2 to max2 etc.
else
        statements
end
```

Note that in the first case, there is no expression after the keyword case. The following shows one example of each of the forms.

```
#Form 1
a = 7
status = case
        when a % 6 != 0 then "not divisible by 6"
        when a % 3 != 0 then "not divisible by 3"
        when a % 2 != 0 then "not divisible by 2"
        else "odd"
end
print status
```

This prints the following.

```
not divisible by 6
```

And this code

```
#Form 2
a = 6
status = case a
        when 1..4,6...10 then "Not equal to 5"
        when 5 then "equal to 5"
        else "above 9"
end
print status
```

prints as follows.

```
Not equal to 5
```

Note that in either case, the condition (from the top) that has first been evaluated to be true has the corresponding statement executed. That is how a case statement works in Ruby.

It is not required if the statement is not on the same line as the condition.

```
a = 7
status = case
        when a > 6
                "more than 6"
        when a > 4
                "more than 4"
        else "less than 5"
end
print status
```

while

Ruby provides looping mechanisms. One such construct is while. This was already discussed in the context of reading from a file (line by line). Such use of while (for reading and processing file data, line by line) is likely to be significant for batch processing. For the sake of completeness, while is of the following form.

```
while condition
        statements
end
```

This is an example.

```
a = 0
while a < 5
        a = a + 1
        print a
end
```

And it prints like this.

12345

break, redo, next

As a looping construct, while can be used with break, redo, and next to conditionally alter the normal flow of the loop.

The break statement terminates the immediate enclosing loop. Control resumes at the next statement following the block. In nested loops, it only breaks out of one nesting of the loop—the one that is immediately enclosing it.

The next statement skips the current execution (from the point of its occurrence to the end of the loop), effectively starting the next iteration (if there is one possible).

The redo statement repeats the loop from the start without re-evaluating the looping condition or fetching the iterator (if that is the case), once again starting the operation for the current iteration in a way.

The following code illustrates the use of break.

```
a = 0
while a < 4
        a = a + 1
        break if a > 2
        puts a
end
```

It prints the following without the line containing the break.

```
1
2
```

It would have printed 3 and 4 also.

```
1
2
3
4
```

The following code illustrates the use of next.

```
a = 0
while a < 4
        a = a + 1
        next if a > 2
        puts a
end
print "after while"
```

It should print like this.

```
1
2
after while
```

The following code uses redo.

```
a = 0
while a < 4
      a = a + 1
      redo if a == 2
      puts a
end
print "after while"
```

It prints like this.

```
1
3
4
after while
```

Note that when a became 2, redo sent the control back to the beginning statement in the (a = a + 1) loop. The statement after redo (the puts) was not executed for that iteration.

until

until has a similar relation to while as unless has to if. The body is executed until the condition becomes true.

The code shown here

```
a = 0
until a > 3
      a = a + 1
      puts a
end
```

prints as follows.

```
1
2
3
4
```

Again, you should be able to achieve anything with while that you can with until.

for

The for loop has already been briefly discussed. The for loop in Ruby is not very dissimilar to that in Java or C. The only difference is that for does not create a new scope for local variables.

This is the usual form.

```
for <iterating variable> in <Range>
     <statements>
end
```

As already discussed, range can be inclusive and exclusive (for end point); hence, this

```
for a in 1...3
     puts a
end
```

prints as follows. It does not print 3 (the range in this case being exclusive.

```
1
2
```

And the code here

```
for b in 'w'..'z'
     print b
end
```

prints as follows.

```
wxyz
```

As you can also see, the range does not need to be numeric.

3.1 Handling Exceptions

Problem

You want to handle any exceptions that occur in your program.

Solution

Use a combination of rescue and ensure. rescue wraps the code for handling errors. However, sometimes it may be necessary to run a piece of code in the end, no matter whether the execution of a block was normal or encountered an exception. (It somewhat corresponds to the finally block in Java.)

ensure comes in handy in such situations. It comes after rescue. The structure may look like the following code.

```
f = File.open("input.txt")
begin
    code for processing
rescue
    code for handling errors
ensure
    f.close unless f.nil?
end
```

An else construct can be used with this. The part of code for the else is executed only if no error has been encountered in the main part (i.e., it is an else to the rescue).

```
f = File.open("input.txt")
begin
    code for processing
rescue
    code for handling errors
ensure
    f.close unless f.nil?
end
```

To raise an exception, raise can be used (in one of three ways).

```
raise
raise "no file found"
raise ArgumentError, "Too big name", caller
```

The first form simply raises the current exception (or a RuntimeError if there is none). The second one creates a new RuntimeError, setting its message to the string that it specifies. The third form uses the first argument to create an exception, sets the message with the second argument, and sets the stack trace to the third argument.

Single Line Rescue

rescue has a single line form, which may be handy for small pieces of code. It is really easy to demonstrate through an example.

Suppose you define an array of two elements and try to multiply the third element (which is non-existent for the array) by 2; it will come up with an error.

```
irb(main):001:0> a = [1,2]
=> [1, 2]
irb(main):002:0> a[2] * 2
NoMethodError: undefined method `*' for nil:NilClass
        from (irb):2
```

You can, however, wrap up the exception with a rescue, as follows.

```
irb(main):003:0> a[2] * 2 rescue 'No such element'
=> "No such element"
irb(main):004:0> a[1] * 2 rescue 'No such element'
=> 4
```

Note that for an existing element, it provides the proper result.

catch and throw

catch and throw come in handy for arbitrarily jumping out of many levels of nesting and so on. catch defines a block with a label. The block executes normally until a throw is encountered.

When Ruby encounters a throw, it zips back up the call stack looking for a catch block with a matching symbol. When it finds it, it unwinds the stack to that point and terminates the block. If throw is called with an optional second parameter, that value is returned as the value of the catch.

This is a simple example.

```
catch (:testit) do
      i = 0
      while i < 5
            i = i + 1
            j = 0
            while j < 5
                  j = j + 1
                  print i.to_s + "," + j.to_s + ": "
                  throw :testit if i * j > 5
            end
      end
end
```

It prints this.

```
1,1: 1,2: 1,3: 1,4: 1,5: 2,1: 2,2: 2,3:
```

You may wish to comment the line containing the throw statement to see what it prints.

3.2 Working with Predefined Variables and Constants

Problem

Ruby has a lot of predefined variables for various purposes. Some of them are quite useful for batch processing.

Solution

Take $@ for instance, which holds an array of stack trace generated by the last exception. The following code provides a small illustration.

```
begin
        raise
rescue
        print $@
end
```

It could run like this.

```
=>ruby test.rb
["test.rb:2:in `<main>'"]=>
```

The following (all read-only and local to the scope) are useful in pattern matching cases.

- $& – The matched string (after a successful pattern match).

- $` – The string preceding the pattern in a successful pattern match.

- $' – The string following the match in a successful pattern match.

- $1 to $9 – The contents of a successive group of matches in a successful pattern match.

- $~ - Local to the scope but not read-only; a Matchdata object that encapsulates the result of a successful pattern match.

The following piece of code illustrates the use of some of these variables.

```
"abracadabra".match(/rac/)
puts $&
puts $`
puts $'
```

It prints the following.

```
rac
ab
adabra
```

So it prints patterns in the string that matches /rac/ (which is the 'rac' part itself), the pattern before 'rac' (which is 'ab'), and the pattern after 'rac'.

Some of the execution environment variables are as follows.

- $0 – The name of the top-level Ruby program being executed (typically, the name of the program file)

- $? – The exit status of the last child process terminated (read-only and local)
- $* – Command-line arguments (a synonym for ARGV)

Here are some of the input output variables.

- $_ – The last line read (scope local to the thread).
- $/ – The input record separator (newline by default). The gets function, for instance, uses this; setting it to nil results in reading an entire file, for example.
- $. – The number of the last line read from the current input file.
- $, – The output separator (string) to methods such as Kernel#print and Array#join.
- $; – The default separator used by String#split.

For a CSV (comma-separated) file, you normally need to specify ',' as the argument to the split (to get different columns). Take the following input (in a file named input.txt), for example.

```
Seattle,is,a,city
Washington,is,a,state
USA,is,a,country
        and the code
infile = File.open 'input.txt','r'
while line = infile.gets
        col = line.split(',')
        puts "#{col[0]} #{col[3]}"
end
infile.close
```

If you change the value of $; appropriately, then you won't have to call split with that argument.

```
$; = ','
infile = File.open 'input.txt','r'
while line = infile.gets
        col = line.split
        puts "#{col[0]} #{col[3]}"
end
infile.close
```

And that prints the following.

```
Seattle city
Washington state
USA country
```

Although it is a simple use case, you may find more ingenious usage for the same.

67

Predefined Constants

There are some predefined constants as well. One such is ARGV, which has already been discussed (in context of command-line arguments). Most of these are perhaps not as interesting or useful as the predefined variables, but include STDIN, STDOUT, STDERR, and RUBY_VERSION, and ENV.

You may want to go into irb, type **ENV**, and press the Return key. The output (which is the environment variables involved in your Ruby programming environment) may be interesting to watch.

3.3 Running OS Commands

Problem

In a batch execution, you want to run something as an OS command (command line), get the output, and process the same in your own way within the script.

Solution

Running an OS command from Ruby is achieved by using back quote delimiters.
For instance, the following code

```
val = `ls *.txt`
print val
```

may come up with something like the following (Note: if you are using Windows, you have to use dir instead of ls, and the output may be different, especially in format.).

```
coord.txt
inplines.txt
input.txt
modcoord.txt
names.txt
outlines.txt
output.txt
```

You may parse this for your particular data of interest.
This feature can be used to great advantage in batch scripting.

3.4 Initializing and Finalizing Code

Problem

You need to do some initializing, (e.g., set the value of a default variable) that works for the entire program, not just a specific code block. The same is true for some finalizing activity.

Solution

One way of accomplishing this is to use BEGIN and END blocks. They are used to set predefined variables for the length of the script, for instance. BEGIN blocks execute prior to the main script body and END blocks execute after the main script body.

```
BEGIN { puts "abc" }
for i in 1..5
        puts i
end
END { puts "def" }
```

The preceding code prints as follows.

```
abc
1
2
3
4
5
def
```

Note that the blocks can be multiline. Also note that there may be multiple BEGIN and END blocks in a program. BEGIN blocks execute in the order of occurrence and END blocks execute in reverse order. (More of this is covered in Recipe 5.3).

3.5 Defining Functions

Problem

How do you define your own functions in Ruby code?

Solution

A simple function in Ruby (without parameters) can be defined as follows.

```
def <method_name>
        <code>
end
```

def and end are keywords, and <code> represents one or more statements. The function may be called simply with the function name (in the same code body). For example,

```
def say_hello
        print "hello world"
end
say_hello
```

when executed, should print the following.

```
hello world
```

The first three lines of code define a function named say_hello, and the fourth line of code calls the function. For calls outside the class, a dot operator is used. You have already seen a lot of examples of this type of call.

By convention, a function defined in a class is referred to as a *method*.

Note that if you put the function call ahead of the definition in the preceding code, that is,

```
say_hello
def say_hello
        print "hello world"
end
```

it will result in an error, as at the point of execution the definition is unknown.

```
NameError: undefined local variable or method `say_hello' for main:Object
```

Functions with Arguments

Functions with arguments may be declared in various forms.

The following code illustrates a function with arguments and call to that.

```
def sum_of (a, b)
        c = a + b
end
d = sum_of 2,2
print d
```

It prints as follows.

```
4
```

Function Arguments with Default Values

The following code illustrates a function definition with arguments having default values.

```
def sum_of (a = 2, b = 3)
        c = a + b
end
d = sum_of 1,1
print d
puts
e = sum_of
print e
```

It prints as follows.

```
2
5
```

Functions with a Variable Number of Arguments

The following code illustrates function definition with variable number of arguments.

```
def count_of (*numbers)
        c = numbers.length
end
d = count_of 1,3,5
print "the count of arguments is " + d.to_s
```

And it prints as shown in the following.

```
the count of arguments is 3
```

Return Value from Functions

A return statement, when specified, may return zero, one, or more expressions or values. Thus everything in the following is valid.

```
return
return 1
return 1,3,4
return 2 + 5
```

In the first, case nil is returned, and in the third case, an array is returned.

```
irb(main):023:0> def chk
irb(main):024:1> return 2,3,4
irb(main):025:1> end
=> :chk
irb(main):026:0> chk
=> [2, 3, 4]
```

Every method in Ruby returns a value by default (even when explicit return is not specified). If a return statement is not specified, the value returned is the value of the last statement.

Hence, the following function returns "xyz".

```
def seeit
  a = 0
  b = 1
  c = a + b
```

```
  "xy" + "z"
end
str = seeit
puts str
```

Recurrence

It is possible to use function recurrence (calling a function from within itself) in Ruby. This has excellent usage in algorithmic programming. One very simple but classic example is finding the factorial of an integer.

```
def factorial(n)
  if n <= 1
        1
  else
      n * factorial(n-1)
  end
end
puts factorial(5)
puts factorial(0)
puts factorial(6)
```

Note, in the preceding code, the factorial function calls itself at one stage. Note also that the recurrence occurs only when the argument, n, is greater than 1. It is also common for a recurring function to have an exit path (otherwise, it will very likely lead to infinite recursion, or crash). This implies the boundary condition, when the recurrence should not be invoked and an alternate path is to be taken. (This usually is the point where the recurrence should end and produce an accumulated result of previous recurrences.)

Programmers with a terser taste in coding might accomplish such recursion in one line of code inside the function and using the ternary operator.

```
def facto(n)
    (n <= 1) ? 1 : n * facto(n-1)
end
puts facto(6)
```

Exercises

Answers are in the appendix.

Exercise 3.1

Remember that for Fibonacci numbers, a particular number is the sum of the last two numbers in the series. Thus, starting with 0 and 1 as the first two numbers, the series would look like this: 0,1,1,2,3,5,8, and so on. Suppose you define the first 0 as the zeroth

Fibonacci number, the first 1 as the first Fibonacci number, and so on. Hence, in this series, the fourth Fibonacci number is 3, and the fifth is 5.

Write a program, which uses a recurring function to calculate the nth Fibonacci number (n being positive integer). Use this function to find the eighth Fibonacci number. Take zeroth and the first Fibonacci number as given.

■ **Tip**   This recursive function has to take two arguments and it has two edge cases (when recurrence should not happen).

Exercise 3.2

From the series of positive integers (starting with 1), find the first integer (programmatically) whose square exceeds 1,000.

Exercise 3.3

Find the sum of all integers from 1 to 100 (excluding 100), which is either divisible by 3 or divisible by 5, but not by both.

CHAPTER 4

■ ■ ■

Collections

A collection in the context of a computer language, intuitively, has the same meaning as a collection is meant in general. For instance, we may say a collection of books (usually to denote a number of books owned by someone or some organization, and possibly kept in the same bookcase or the same room). So a collection is really a few things of the same type or a similar type of object (numbers, strings, or some other type of objects could also be basic types in some language) taken together. The really important thing to know is why they deserve special mention/special handling in a computer language or computer language learning context.

Before answering that question in my own way, here are a few points about collections (henceforth, a *collection* applies to the computer language context):

- A collection can be empty or have one or more elements in it.

- The collection is usually of a specific type, but may also be of objects that derive from the same type. Since many languages have a base type denoting any object, it is possible that a collection of that type (if allowed in the language) could hold objects of almost any type (because all of the types are derived from the base type). In a real-world analogy, a collection of tigers is more specific than a collection of animals, which includes many types of animals.

- As mentioned, a collection can be basic types (such as int in Java). Note that in Ruby, even basic types are actually objects.

- The way collections differ (and this is a very general way to look at it) is usually the way the elements are relatively organized within the collection. In a real-world analogy, you can throw some marbles in a bag, but in a study table, you may stack books, one on top of another. (They may be considered different arrangements, and hence, different types of collections).

Now, what is it about a collection that deserves special mention or special treatment? In a real-world analogy, why would something about a collection of books be a very different concern from the books themselves?

© Malay Mandal 2016
M. Mandal, *Ruby Recipes*, DOI 10.1007/978-1-4842-2469-4_4

The answer lies in the *relative arrangement* (a.k.a. the organization of the collection). This also affects how you put it in a particular place (considering it is organized in a certain way) and how you retrieve a particular object from a collection.

In a good library, for instance, the books could be organized in such a way that searching for a certain title in a catalog or other reference points you to the exact location of the book (including the section, the rack, and so on). It can also tell you if the book has been borrowed and is not currently in library. This organization is unlikely to have any connection to the detailed content of a particular book; it usually only deals with the title, category, author, and such.

In a computing context, a collection is more about the relative arrangement and organization of objects, largely keeping in view the ease of storage, search, and retrieval of items in the collection, rather than being preoccupied with a particular item. It can also provide useful information about the collection (as a group), such as whether it is empty, how many objects it has, and so on.

An *array* (a type of collection), for instance, organizes its objects in a numeric index. It is like giving you a key to a locker within a series of lockers and with the number of the particular locker. So that when you have to open, for instance, locker number 5, you can go straight to the fifth locker and open it. What is kept in the locker is usually not the concern of the people who have rented you the locker. (Although, you may have to sign some declaration that you won't be keeping explosives or hazardous material inside).

Ruby has a few types of collections, such as arrays, hashes, and sets. They are discussed in some detail in this chapter.

4.1 Creating and Initializing Arrays

Problem

How do you create an array in Ruby?

Solution

In Ruby, arrays are sequentially an integer-indexed collection of objects. The starting index is 0 (like C or Java), however a negative index is considered from the end (in reverse), with –1 referring to the last element.

Arrays can hold strings, integers, hashes, and so on (including other arrays). *Ruby arrays can grow automatically as needed.*

There are many ways to create an array in Ruby. One option may be more suitable than the others, based on the situation. An array can be created using literals, which in this case is a list of 0 or more objects within square brackets, or by explicitly instantiating an Array object.

Many valid ways of creating/initializing an array, are shown next.

```
a1 = []
puts a1.length
```

A new array, a1, is created. The length function, called on an array, indicates the number of elements that the array has at that point. In this case, the code would print 0, because it is an empty array.

For initializing the array with a number of elements, as it is created, you could use the following.

```
a1 = [1,2,5]
...
a2 = Array.new
```

This creates an empty array.

```
...
a3 = Array.new(20)
puts a3.length
```

An array of size 20 is created (the length is 20), with all elements initialized to nil.

```
...
a4 = Array.new(4,"a")
```

This creates an array of size 4 and initializes all elements to "a", as you can see.

```
irb(main):007:0> a4 = Array.new(4,"a")
=> ["a", "a", "a", "a"]
...
irb(main):001:0> a6 = Array.[](1,2,3,4,5)
=> [1, 2, 3, 4, 5]
...
irb(main):002:0> a7 = Array[1,2,3,4,5]
=> [1, 2, 3, 4, 5]
...
a8 = Array(0..9)
```

Now you can use a range to initialize an array.

```
irb(main):003:0> a8 = Array(0..9)
=> [0, 1, 2, 3, 4, 5, 6, 7, 8, 9]
...
```

For a Ruby array it is legal to hold multiple types of objects at the same time. Thus, the following is perfectly legal in Ruby.

```
a1 = [1,"cat",2,"dog",3]
```

4.2 Accessing Array Elements

Problem

You want to access the elements in an array.

Solution

Arrays are organized linearly with numeric indices. In Ruby (as in many other languages), the index of the first element is 0, the second element is 1, and so on.

The element at index j (which is actually *j+1-th* element) is accessed as <array-name>[j]. That is, for the following array a1, the first element (whose value is 1) can be accessed as a1[0], the second element ("cat") can be accessed as a1[1], and so on.

```
a1 = [1,"cat",2,"dog",3]

irb(main):002:0> a1[0]
=> 1
irb(main):003:0> a1[1]
=> "cat"
```

Note that trying to access an index that is out of bounds for the array does not result in an error, but returns nil.

```
irb(main):004:0> a1[6]
=> nil
...
```

Unlike many other computer languages, Ruby allows negative array indices. They denote elements from the last position, backward; the last position index being –1.

Hence, in the preceding array, a1[-1] refers to 3 (the last element) and a1[-2] refers to "dog" (the last element).

```
a1 = [1,"cat",2,"dog",3]
puts "last element : " + a1[-1].to_s
puts "element before last : " + a1[-2].to_s
```

It prints like this:

```
last element : 3
element before last : dog
```

(Note that for puts, the non-string elements had to be converted with to_s).

It is possible to access part of the array in an array[start,length] style index range or an array[Range] style index range. Here is an example.

```
a1 = [1,"cat",2,"dog",3]
print a1[1,2]
puts
print a1[1..3]
```

This prints as follows.

```
["cat", 2]
["cat", 2, "dog"]
```

4.3 Inserting an Element at a Certain Position

Problem

You want to insert elements into an array at a certain position.

Solution

It can be done by assigning the new value to the element, by *referring the element with its index*. It is possible to assign values to multiple elements at the same time (using the same principle of access, such as range and so forth, as already discussed).

The following code illustrates various assignments on array elements.

```
a1 = [1,"cat",2,"dog",3]
a1[5] = 'tiger'  # added at the end
# now array is [1, "cat", 2, "dog", 3, "tiger"]
print a1
puts
a1[3] = 'wolf'  #1 element gets replaced
# now array is [1, "cat", 2, "wolf", 3, "tiger"]
print a1
puts
a1[2,2] = [4,'bat'] # 2 elements gets replaced by 2 new ones
# now array is [1, "cat", 4, "bat", 3, "tiger"]
print a1
puts
a1[2,2] = 'possam' # 2 elements gets replaced by 1 new element, array
shrinks
# now array is [1, "cat", "possam", 3, "tiger"]
print a1
puts
```

```
a1[2,1] = [5,'lynx'] # one element gets replaced by 2 , array grows
# now array is [1, "cat", 5, "lynx", 3, "tiger"]
print a1
puts
a1[-4..-3] = [2,'dog'] # replace using range
# now array is [1, "cat", 2, "dog", 3, "tiger"]
print a1
...
```

4.4 Working with Multidimensional Arrays

Problem

You want to work with data that requires a multidimensional array.

Solution

Multidimensional arrays are somewhat counterintuitive in Ruby. They should simply be declared as an array of arrays (or an array of an array of arrays, and so on), and the dimensions are not consistent. (An array may have one element as single and another element as an array).

Here is an illustrative example.

```
a = [1,[2,3]]
```

As you can see, this is not something that you would expect in Java. But it is valid.

```
b = [[1,2,3],[4,5,6]]
```

This is more organized. Note that in this case, the way to access an element is very similar to many other languages.

```
b[1][0]  => 4
```

However weird it might seem, Ruby multidimensional arrays can be worked upon interestingly. The transpose and flatten functions are notable.

```
irb(main):005:0> a.flatten
=> [1, 2, 3]
irb(main):006:0> b.transpose
=> [[1, 4], [2, 5], [3, 6]]
```

Note that flatten has an in place version, flatten!, which changes the original array rather than returning a new modified copy. (In place operations are discussed in Recipe 4.5.)

4.5 Working with Arrays

Problem

You want to use the full set of array operations, such as getting information about an array, comparing arrays, and carrying out set operations.

Solution

The Array class has plenty of methods (some inherited) to facilitate working with arrays.

You might already have seen the length function. A similar function is size, which returns the (current) size of the array.

The following prints a 5.

```
a = [2,3,5,4,1]
print a.size
```

empty?

empty? checks whether an array is empty or otherwise.

```
irb(main):001:0> a = []
=> []
irb(main):002:0> b = [1,2]
=> [1, 2]
irb(main):003:0> a.empty?
=> true
irb(main):004:0> b.empty?
=> false
```

fill

fill can fill an array partially or fully (based on how it is used). It has many forms. Some forms are shown in following example.

```
irb(main):001:0> a = Array.new(5)
=> [nil, nil, nil, nil, nil]
irb(main):002:0> a.fill('x')
=> ["x", "x", "x", "x", "x"]
irb(main):003:0> a.fill('y',2,2)
=> ["x", "x", "y", "y", "x"]
irb(main):004:0> a.fill('z',1..2)
=> ["x", "z", "z", "y", "x"]
```

Add, Subtract, Compare, and Contrast

Linear (a.k.a. one-dimensional) arrays can be worked upon in Ruby with some functions, which may have a feel of arithmetic fluidity.

+

The + concatenates two arrays.

```
irb(main):001:0> [1,2,3] + [4,5]
=> [1, 2, 3, 4, 5]
```

concat

The concat function can also be used to similar effect as +.

-

The - function

```
irb(main):002:0> [1,2,3,4,5] - [2,3]
=> [1, 4, 5]
```

The behavior of - is somewhat like a set operation. It doesn't affect non-existing elements in the first array, and removes repeated elements when required.

```
irb(main):003:0> [1,2,2,4,5,5] - [2,3]
=> [1, 4, 5, 5]
```

*

The * function has repetitive action.

```
irb(main):004:0> [3,4] * 3
=> [3, 4, 3, 4, 3, 4]
```

<<

The << function appends an element or array at the end of the left array.

```
irb(main):006:0> [1,2] << 'a'
=> [1, 2, "a"]
irb(main):007:0> [2,3] << 'a' << 'b' << [4,5]
=> [2, 3, "a", "b", [4, 5]]
```

==

The == function checks the equality of two arrays (alternatively, the eql? method can be used).

```
irb(main):008:0> [1,2] == [1, 2]
=> true
irb(main):009:0> [1,2] == [2,3]
=> false
```

<=>

The <=> function is the comparison operator. Returns an integer (-1, 0, or 1 based on whether the first array is less than, equal to, or greater than the second array).

```
irb(main):010:0> ['a','a','b'] <=> ['a','b','c']
=> -1
irb(main):011:0> [4,5,6] <=> [2,3]
=> 1
irb(main):012:0> ['a','a','b'] <=> ['a','b']
=> -1
```

Set Operations

An array, as a collection, is not a set in mathematical sense. In a more general sense (i.e., in the English-language term), it can be thought of as a set of things (of course, structured in a certain manner). From that point of view, you can think of a set operation between two arrays as a set operation between two sets of things.

At a conceptual level, set operations on arrays in general work on the set of elements of one array with those of another array. If there is a common element in both arrays, for instance (whether it occurs once, or multiple times, in either array), this is returned as part of the output of intersection operation of those two arrays. Some of these operations are described next.

| (or union)

```
irb(main):013:0> ['a','a','b'] | ['b','c','c','d']
=> ["a", "b", "c", "d"]
```

Note that duplicate elements are eliminated.

& (or intersection)

```
irb(main):014:0> ['a','a','b','b','c'] & ['b','c','c','d']
=> ["b", "c"]
```

uniq

As a side note, you can use the union operation with an empty array to get an array with a unique set of elements.

```
irb(main):016:0> ['a','a','b','b','c'] | []
=> ["a", "b", "c"]
```

But a cleaner way to do that is using the uniq function.

```
irb(main):017:0> ['a','a','b','b','c'].uniq
=> ["a", "b", "c"]
```

In Place Operations

This is a common feature of Ruby (not just restricted to arrays). A function that has a ! at the end usually denotes an in place operation (meaning it changes the original array, as opposed to returning a new modified copy, keeping the original intact). For instance, uniq has a variation, which is uniq!, and that works in place (i.e., on the original array).

```
irb(main):001:0> a = ['a','a','b','b','c']
=> ["a", "a", "b", "b", "c"]
irb(main):002:0> b = a.uniq
=> ["a", "b", "c"]
irb(main):003:0> print a
["a", "a", "b", "b", "c"]=> nil
irb(main):004:0> c = a.uniq!
=> ["a", "b", "c"]
irb(main):005:0> print a
["a", "b", "c"]=> nil
```

Note that similar to this, if a method name ends in ? (e.g., eql?), it usually checks the trueness of something and returns a Boolean value.

There are other utilities, notably sort and reverse, which also have in place versions.

sort (and sort!)

sort and sort! are used to sort the elements of an array. It is very handy for a lot of scripting tasks.

```
irb(main):006:0> [1,3,4,2,6,3,9,5,4].sort
=> [1, 2, 3, 3, 4, 4, 5, 6, 9]
```

Note that sort has another form, which uses the block feature of Ruby (discussed in Recipe 5.4).

reverse (and reverse!)

reverse! does the same thing but on the original array itself.

```
irb(main):007:0> [1, 2, 3, 3, 4, 4, 5, 6, 9].reverse
=> [9, 6, 5, 4, 4, 3, 3, 2, 1]
```

Further Access and Manipulation

A few more useful functions of Array API are explained next.

include?

As you can see, the include? method ends in a ?, which checks whether a certain element is contained in an array (and returns a boolean value). It is like the contains function in some languages.

```
irb(main):008:0> ['a','b','c'].include?('d')
=> false
irb(main):009:0> ['a','b','c'].include?('c')
=> true
```

index

You can get the index of a particular element within an array, using the index method (given the element value). It is a somewhat counterintuitive approach to lookup an array, but it can be very useful sometimes.

```
irb(main):010:0> ['a','b','b','c','d'].index('c')
=> 3
irb(main):011:0> ['a','b','b','c','d'].index('b')
=> 1
```

Note that for repetitive elements, it returns the index of the first occurrence. It returns nil if the element does not exist in the array.

rindex

rindex a function similar to index, but it returns the rightmost index (in a repetitive element) or nil if it does not exist.

```
irb(main):001:0> ['a','b','b','c','d'].rindex('b')
=> 2
irb(main):002:0> ['a','b','b','c','d'].rindex('e')
=> nil
```

85

values_at

You can access the elements of an array using <array>[start-index,length] or <array>[range] construct. But both of these require that the elements be returned to a contiguous position. If you need to return an array (a subarray of the original) with multiple elements but not contiguous, you can use the values_at function.

```
irb(main):001:0> ['a','b','d','f','j','l','m'].values_at(0,2,5)
=> ["a", "d", "l"]
```

fetch

fetch is for accessing an element of an array. However, it can be more useful than a normal access mechanism when the index may be out of bounds and that should not cause an exception in the flow of execution. It has a few forms (two of them are discussed here).

A fetch without argument returns the element at that index or results in an error for out-of-bound indexes.

```
irb(main):008:0> a1 = [1,"cat",2,"dog",3]
=> [1, "cat", 2, "dog", 3]
irb(main):009:0> a1.fetch(0)
=> 1
irb(main):010:0> a1.fetch(6)
IndexError: index 6 outside of array bounds: -5...5
        from (irb):10:in `fetch'
        from (irb):10
```

However, a fetch with an argument returns the argument as an alternate value in *index out of bounds* cases.

```
irb(main):011:0> a1.fetch(6,'Not found')
=> "Not found"
```

insert

The insert function allows insertion at a certain index position (pushing later elements to higher index positions to create space). It is possible to insert multiple elements at once. It is also possible to use a negative index (–1 is the last item, –2 is the item before that, and so on).

```
irb(main):002:0> a = ['a','b','c','d']
=> ["a", "b", "c", "d"]
irb(main):003:0> a.insert(2,5)
=> ["a", "b", 5, "c", "d"]
```

```
irb(main):004:0> a.insert(-2,6)
=> ["a", "b", 5, "c", 6, "d"]
irb(main):005:0> a.insert(4, 'e','f')
=> ["a", "b", 5, "c", "e", "f", 6, "d"]
```

Note that it affects the original array.

delete

delete deletes all occurrences of a specified item from the array. It returns nil if the item is not found.

```
irb(main):007:0> a = ['a','b','b','c','d']
=> ["a", "b", "b", "c", "d"]
irb(main):008:0> a.delete('b')
=> "b"
irb(main):009:0> print a
["a", "c", "d"]=> nil
irb(main):010:0> a.delete('z')
=> nil
```

In the return of the print a command in irb (shown earlier), note that first the value of the a array at that point is printed. Then, the return value (of print function) is printed after the =>. Since the print function returns nil (it prints to the console, but returns nil), that part turns up as => nil.

The delete function has another form that can return something other than nil and that uses the block feature.

```
irb(main):011:0> a.delete('z') { 'Value not in array' }
=> "Value not in array"
```

delete_at

delete_at is used to delete elements at a particular index. For an out of range index, it returns nil.

```
irb(main):001:0> a = ['a','b','c','d','e']
=> ["a", "b", "c", "d", "e"]
irb(main):002:0> a.delete_at(2)
=> "c"
irb(main):003:0> print a
["a", "b", "d", "e"]=> nil
```

join

join returns a string, which is made by joining all the elements (using a specific separator between elements, if one is given). The default separator is $, which is usually nil.

```
irb(main):005:0> ['n','o','t','e'].join
=> "note"
irb(main):006:0> ['abra','ca','dabra'].join('-')
=> "abra-ca-dabra"
```

compact

compact removes nil elements from array and collapses it (if there was any nil element to begin with).

```
irb(main):007:0> ['a',nil,nil,'b',nil,'c'].compact
=> ["a", "b", "c"]
```

clear

clear removes all elements from the array.

```
irb(main):008:0> a = ['x','y','z']
=> ["x", "y", "z"]
irb(main):009:0> a.clear
=> []
```

4.6 Creating Hashes

Problem

How is a hash created in Ruby?

Solution

Hashes (also known as *associative arrays* or *maps*) are a collection of key-value pairs. The keys are not necessarily numeric or sequential; however, they should be unique across the hash. The values are retrieved through the corresponding keys.

A hash is structured/organized like this:

```
["cat" => "feline", "wolf" => "lupine", "bear" => "ursine"]
```

And instead of retrieving an element in this way, for example—'element at index 0', it is retrieved like this: 'element whose key is "wolf"'.

A key can be any Ruby object (even an array); however, a string key is quite common.

A hash can be created in many ways. The following are some examples.

```
h1 = Hash.new
```

This creates an empty hash:

```
h2 = Hash['a' => 100, 'b' => 200]
```

This creates a hash and initializes it with two key-value pairs. At this point, if h2 is printed, it would look like this:

```
{"a"=>100, "b"=>200}
```

And the elements can be accessed as h['a'] or h['b'].

```
irb(main):003:0> h2['a']
=> 100
irb(main):004:0> h2['b']
=> 200
```

The following works.

```
h = Hash["a" => 100, "b" => 200]
```

And so does the following.

```
h = { "a" => 100, "b" => 200 }
```

A hash can be created with a default value (as shown in the following).

```
h = Hash.new ('unknown')
```

The significance of the default value is that, if it is accessed with a key, which is non-existent for the hash, then the default value will be returned. (For a hash, where no default value is available, it returns nil in such situations).

4.7 Adding New Elements to a Hash

Problem

How do you add new elements to an existing hash?

Solution

After a new hash is created with a default value, let's say as follows...

```
h = Hash.new('unknown')
```

The addition of new entries can be done by assigning a value to a new key position, as shown here.

```
h['AUS'] = 'Canberra'
h['UK'] = 'London'
h['JP'] = 'Tokyo'
```

At this point, the hash's length or size is 3.

```
irb(main):005:0> h.length
=> 3
irb(main):006:0> h.size
=> 3
```

However, if a key, which is non-existent, is accessed, it returns the default value.

```
irb(main):007:0> h['USA']
=> "unknown"
```

The default values can be accessed by the default method at any point.

```
irb#1(main):017:0> h.default
=> "unknown"
```

And they are set with the default= method.

```
irb#1(main):018:0> h.default='ABCD'
=> "ABCD"
irb#1(main):019:0> h['x']
=> "ABCD"
```

But more importantly, the set of keys and the values of a hash can be accessed using the keys and values methods, respectively.

```
irb#1(main):014:0> h.keys
=> ["AUS", "UK", "JP"]
irb#1(main):015:0> h.values
=> ["Canberra", "London", "Tokyo"]
```

The set of keys for a hash in particular is important for iterating through its elements.

4.8 Working with Hashes

Problem

You want to use the full set of hash operations, such as getting information about a hash, inverting a hash, and accessing data in a hash.

Solution

The Hash class in Ruby offers a rich set of functions. Some of these have already been discussed. In fact, the access operator [ ] (e.g., h['a']) and the assignment operator [ ]= (e.g., h['a'] = 1) are themselves methods. More methods are discussed next.

clear

clear clears a hash (removes all its elements). Note that it works in place (i.e., on the original hash object).

```
irb(main):001:0> h = { 1 => 'a', 2 => 'b' }
=> {1=>"a", 2=>"b"}
irb(main):002:0> h.clear
=> {}
irb(main):003:0> print h
{}=> nil
```

empty?

empty? checks whether the hash is empty or not. It returns a Boolean.

```
irb(main):004:0> h.empty?
=> true
```

has_key?

has_key? checks whether the given key exists in the hash. It returns a Boolean. The same function is called with other names, such as – key?, include?, member?.

```
irb(main):005:0> h = { 1 => 'a', 2 => 'b' }
=> {1=>"a", 2=>"b"}
irb(main):006:0> h.has_key?(1)
=> true
irb(main):007:0> h.has_key?(3)
=> false
```

This is a very useful function to work with a hash.

has_value?

has_value? is the counterpart of the has_key? function for checking the existence of a given value in the hash. It also has a synonym: value?.

```
irb(main):008:0> h.has_value?('b')
=> true
irb(main):009:0> h.has_value?('c')
=> false
```

key

key is used to get the key of a given value. It returns `nil` if the value is not present in the hash.

```
irb(main):001:0> { 1 => 'a', 2 => 'b' }.key('b')
=> 2
irb(main):002:0> { 1 => 'a', 2 => 'b' }.key('c')
=> nil
```

fetch

A `fetch` has a similar connotation to the function with same name in array. It accesses an element of a hash. This can be more useful than a normal access mechanism when there is a possibility that the key, for which the element is being attempted to be retrieved, may not be present in the hash and that should not cause an exception.

A `fetch` without argument returns the element for that key or results in an error, if the key is not present. But a `fetch` with a second argument, returns the value specified in that argument when the key is not present.

```
irb(main):001:0> { 1 => 'a', 2 => 'b' }.fetch(2,'invalid key')
=> "b"
irb(main):002:0> { 1 => 'a', 2 => 'b' }.fetch(3,'invalid key')
=> "invalid key"
```

values_at

Somewhat similar to its namesake in array, `values_at` can retrieve values for multiple keys in one shot.

```
irb(main):003:0> h = {1 => 'a',2 => 'b',3 => 'c',4 => 'd'}
=> {1=>"a", 2=>"b", 3=>"c", 4=>"d"}
irb(main):004:0> h.values_at(1,4)
=> ["a", "d"]
irb(main):005:0> h.values_at(2,5)
=> ["b", nil]
```

Note that it returns `nil` for non-existent keys. For a hash with a default value, it returns the default value in those places.

```
irb(main):006:0> h.default = 'x'
=> "x"
irb(main):007:0> h.values_at(2,5,8)
=> ["b", "x", "x"]
```

delete

The delete function deletes the value in the given key and returns the value (or returns nil if a key is not present). This function has more than one form.

```
irb(main):008:0> {1 => 'a', 2 => 'b'}.delete(1)
=> "a"
irb(main):009:0> {1 => 'a', 2 => 'b'}.delete(3)
=> nil
```

invert

invert returns a new hash, which is an inversion of the original hash (in the sense that the values of the original hash are made keys to this hash, and the corresponding keys of the original hash are made corresponding values). This can be very useful sometimes.

```
irb(main):010:0> {1 => 'a', 2 => 'b'}.invert
=> {"a"=>1, "b"=>2}
```

to_a

to_a converts the hash into a two-dimensional array, where each internal array is a conversion of the key-value pairs of the hash.

```
irb(main):013:0> {1 => 'a', 2 => 'b'}.to_a
=> [[1, "a"], [2, "b"]]
```

==

== compares two hashes for equality. It returns a Boolean.

```
irb(main):001:0> {1 => 'a', 2 => 'b'} == {1 => 'a', 3 => 'c'}
=> false
irb(main):002:0> {1 => 'a', 2 => 'b'} == {1 => 'a', 2 => 'b'}
=> true
irb(main):003:0> {1 => 'a', 2 => 'b'} == {2 => 'b', 1 => 'a'}
=> true
```

merge (and merge!)

Called on one hash, with another hash object as argument, the merge function returns a new hash (merge! is the in place version) that merges the elements of the second hash to the first hash. Any common key gets the value of the second hash. (This function also has another form involving the block feature).

```
irb(main):007:0> h1 = {1 => 'a', 2 => 'b'}
=> {1=>"a", 2=>"b"}
irb(main):008:0> h2 = {1 => 'd', 3 => 'c'}
=> {1=>"d", 3=>"c"}
irb(main):009:0> h1.merge(h2)
=> {1=>"d", 2=>"b", 3=>"c"}
```

4.9 Creating a Collection of Unique Objects

Problem

You want to create a collection of unique objects.

Solution

A *set* is a common type of collection. A Ruby set (which intuitively points to a collection of objects), follows a somewhat mathematical (set theory) convention:

- Each object in a set may occur only once.

- There is no specific ordering or indexing in a set.

Sets can be very useful for many algorithms, where something needs to be represented as a collection of unique objects.

In Ruby, in order to use a set, you need to include the corresponding module (actually require works at the file level, so it includes the set.rb file). The following code shows how to create a set and add elements to it, as well as initializing a set with multiple elements at creation.

```
#include the corresponding module
require 'set'
#create an empty set
s1 = Set.new
#add elements to the set
s1.add(1)
s1.add('a')
#create and initialise a set
s2 = Set.new [1,2,'c'] #use at least one space between new and [
s3 = [1,2,'d'].to_set
```

Note that a set can contain multiple types of elements. (*Note also that for the second form—that is the definition for* s2, *there has to be at least one space between new and the opening square bracket*; otherwise, it will result in an error).

Possibly the easiest way (in terms of typing), however, is to use the Set[ ] construct directly.

```
irb(main):004:0> require 'set'
=> true
irb(main):005:0> Set[1,2]
=> #<Set: {1, 2}>
```

Note that even in irb, you need to require it once for the session.

There is no question of retrieving an individual element of a set (unlike an array or a hash), because individual elements do not have an identity as such within the organization of the set. However, set operations (in a mathematical sense) can be performed on the set, with other sets, and there are ways to determine whether a particular elements exists in the set or not (without any such operation, defining a set would be meaningless anyway).

4.10 Inspecting a Set

Problem

You want to see what is in a set.

Solution

A good way to inspect the current contents of a set is to use the p function, as shown next.

```
irb(main):001:0> require 'set'
=> true
irb(main):002:0> s = Set.new [1,2,'c']
=> #<Set: {1, 2, "c"}>
irb(main):003:0> p s
#<Set: {1, 2, "c"}>
=> #<Set: {1, 2, "c"}>
irb(main):004:0> print s
#<Set:0x007fd019976b20>=> nil
```

Note that p (a bit like print or puts but not quite), prints the value to be inspected rather than invoking to_s on the object (as puts or print does). Hence, if to_s is not defined/overridden in the class satisfactorily, then it may print the object-id, and so forth (see the output of print s in the preceding case).

4.11 Working with Sets

Problem

You want to use the full set of set operations, such as getting information about a hash, inverting a hash, and accessing data in a hash.

Solution

The Set API provides a rich set of functions to manipulate a single set, perform set operations on two sets, and so on. Some of these functions are discussed next.

Checking and Changing

Let's start with the set [1,2].

```
irb(main):002:0> s = Set[1,2]
=> #<Set: {1, 2}>
```

length (or size)

length or size provides the size of the set (in terms of the number of elements).

```
irb(main):003:0> s.length
=> 2
irb(main):004:0> s.size
=> 2
```

empty?

empty? checks if the set is empty. It returns a Boolean.

```
irb(main):005:0> s.empty?
=> false
```

include?

include? checks if the given item exists in the set. It returns a Boolean.

```
irb(main):006:0> s.include?(1)
=> true
```

clear

clear removes all elements from the set.

```
irb(main):007:0> s.clear
=> #<Set: {}>
```

<< (or add)

<< adds an element in the set.

```
irb(main):009:0> s << 'a'
=> #<Set: {"a"}>
```

merge

merge can be used to add multiple elements at the same time.

```
irb(main):011:0> s.merge(['b','c','d','e','f'])
=> #<Set: {"a", "b", "c", "d", "e", "f"}>
```

delete

delete is used to delete one item.

```
irb(main):013:0> s.delete('a')
=> #<Set: {"b", "c", "d", "e", "f"}>
```

Note that it returns the remaining set.

subtract

subtract deletes multiple items at the same time.

```
irb(main):014:0> s.subtract(['c','d'])
=> #<Set: {"b", "e", "f"}>
```

Note that change is done to the original set (see the following).

```
irb(main):015:0> p s
#<Set: {"b", "e", "f"}>
=> #<Set: {"b", "e", "f"}>
```

Also note that for partial existence in the delete list (i.e., the argument to subtract contains some elements that do not exist in the first set), only the elements that exist in the original set will be deleted.

```
irb(main):016:0> s.subtract(['e','g'])
=> #<Set: {"b", "f"}>
```


==

The == function checks the equality of two sets.

```
irb(main):018:0> s2 = Set[2,3]
=> #<Set: {2, 3}>
irb(main):019:0> s3 = Set[3,2]
=> #<Set: {3, 2}>
irb(main):020:0> s2 == s3
=> true
```

Note that the order of the elements does not matter.

Set Operations

The Set API provides many functions.

+ (or | or union)

The + or | functions return a set that is the union of two sets.

```
irb(main):022:0> s1 = Set[1,2,3,4]
=> #<Set: {1, 2, 3, 4}>
irb(main):023:0> s2 = Set[3,4,5,6]
=> #<Set: {3, 4, 5, 6}>
irb(main):024:0> s1 + s2
=> #<Set: {1, 2, 3, 4, 5, 6}>
```

& (or intersection)

The & function returns the intersection of two sets.
    (Assume the preceding two sets, s1 and s2, are in scope.)

```
irb(main):025:0> s1 & s2
=> #<Set: {3, 4}>
```

intersect?

The intersect? function checks whether two sets intersect (i.e., if there is any common element at all). It returns a Boolean.

```
irb(main):026:0> s1.intersect?(s2)
=> true
```

disjoint?

The disjoint? function checks whether two sets are disjoint. Two sets are disjoint if they have no elements in common. (It is essentially the exact opposite of intersect?).

```
irb(main):027:0> s1.disjoint?(s2)
=> false
```

- (or difference)

The - function shows the differences between two sets. It returns a set contain any element that is in the first set but not in the second.

```
irb(main):028:0> s1 - s2
=> #<Set: {1, 2}>
```

^

The ^ provides a set that contains elements from both sets, but not the common elements.

```
irb(main):029:0> s1 ^ s2
=> #<Set: {5, 6, 1, 2}>
```

Subset and superset

If s1 and s2 are sets that are defined as follows

```
irb(main):030:0> s1 = Set[1,2,3]
=> #<Set: {1, 2, 3}>
irb(main):031:0> s2 = Set[1,2]
=> #<Set: {1, 2}>
```

the verification of whether s1 is a *superset* of s2 is done by using the >= function.

```
irb(main):032:0> s1 >= s2
=> true
```

The same effect can be achieved with the superset? function.

```
irb(main):034:0> s1.superset?(s2)
=> true
```

Note that any set is a subset of itself, and hence s1 >= s1 is true.

```
irb(main):033:0> s1 >= s1
=> true
```

However, s1 is a proper superset of s1 in this case (a proper superset of a set should be a superset of the set, but should have at least one more element than the corresponding subset), but s1 cannot be a proper superset of itself. To check whether a set (s1) is a proper superset of another set (s2) is done with the > function, as shown next.

```
irb(main):035:0> s1 > s2
=> true
irb(main):036:0> s1 > s1
=> false
```

There is a corresponding proper_superset? function to check the same.
There are also corresponding functions—such as subset?, proper_subset?, <, and <= —that check the inverse relationship.

```
irb(main):038:0> s1 <= s1
=> true
irb(main):039:0> s2 <= s1
=> true
irb(main):040:0> s2.proper_subset?(s1)
=> true
irb(main):041:0> s2 < s1
=> true
```

Flattening and Conversion

A set of sets can be flattened by using the flatten function. (The in place counterpart is flatten?).

```
irb(main):050:0> s = Set[Set[1,2], Set[3,4], Set[2,3], Set[4,5]]
=> #<Set: {#<Set: {1, 2}>, #<Set: {3, 4}>, #<Set: {2, 3}>, #<Set: {4, 5}>}>
irb(main):051:0> s.flatten!
=> #<Set: {1, 2, 3, 4, 5}>
```

A set can be converted to an array using the to_a function.

```
irb(main):055:0> Set['a','c','b','e','d'].to_a
=> ["a", "c", "b", "e", "d"]
```

Collections will be brought up again in context of iterators. But before beginning on blocks and iterators, you may wish to try some exercises.

Exercises

The solutions are in the appendix.

Exercise 4.1

Given an array of letters and a word as input, write a program to find out whether the word can be built from the letters contained in the array. Any letter can be used up to as many times as it occurs in the array (i.e., if the word needs three letter a's, then the array should have at least three letter a's).

Using the program (/) function, show that for the array ['y','z','b','e','a','u','t'] and the word *beauty* returns true, but ['r','o','u','g','h'] and *tough* returns false.

Exercise 4.2

Suppose there are two text files that report train timing (in a 24-hour format). The first report provides arrival times to a station (on a particular day), and the second report provides departure times. The file contents are as follows.

arrtime.txt

```
43UP  8:35
54DN  10:32
32UP  11:52
10DN  13:56
45DN  14:20
```

deptime.txt

```
54DN  11:14
45DN  14:28
43UP  8:30
10DN  13:59
35UP  11:52
```

The data is space separated. The first column is the train number (train id) and the second column is the time. The data is not ordered by train id.

Note that the data may have an anomaly, such as the arrival may be later than the departure, and also one train id may be found in one file, but not another.

The exercise is to programmatically find the amount of time (in minutes) that each train stays in the station (when possible), and to flag the trains that have data anomalies.

CHAPTER 5

■ ■ ■

Blocks and Iterators

Intuitively, a block of code is a set of statements that are grouped together. For instance, statements within a function (function body) or the block of code to be executed inside the while loop. However, Ruby has a special block feature that (while still being a group of one or more statements usually enclosed in flower brackets) has very interesting usages. It is especially useful in the context of iterator methods for collections.

Perhaps it is best to explain by example to a Ruby newbie.

First of all, a block (and this refers to the block feature, not just any general block of code) can be any chunk of code bounded by do-end keyword pairs or { }. The following are both valid blocks.

```
do
        puts "Hello"
        puts "world"
end
```

and

```
{ puts 'hello world' }
```

And while they have a somewhat anonymous function feel about them, these code bodies, by themselves, will not run.

Try the following, however; it will work.

```
3.times do
        puts 'Hello'
end
```

And it prints this:

```
Hello
Hello
Hello
```

There is a convention (but not a syntactic rule) that do-end is preferred in multiline code over {}. (Note that henceforth in the book, the {} variation is usually used rather than the do-end variety).

© Malay Mandal 2016
M. Mandal, *Ruby Recipes*, DOI 10.1007/978-1-4842-2469-4_5

What happened here?

The number 3 is a Fixnum object on which the times method has been called. The block (beginning with do and ending with end) has been passed as an argument to the times method. The code block argument has been executed that many times.

times here is an iterator method that takes a block as an argument and executes it repeatedly (the number of repetitions depends on the context).

5.1 Associating Blocks with Functions

Problem

Suppose you have a rather long function in which you are to repeatedly perform a set of actions on a variable (or variables) as it changes its state through the course of the function. Think of putting debug messages, which prints the variable name, its current value, and also some kind of marker that indicates the relative position of this message within the function. For example, printing messages like this:

```
X is now 3 before the iteration
X is now 5 inside the if statement
```

It would be nice if you could pass the value of x and the position marker string (e.g., "before the iteration" or "inside the if statement") and that subfunction, called from the right places, prints those messages nicely for you.

Using a separate function for that purpose seems a bit heavy-handed. Besides, your project may have policies against creating debug functions for deliverable code. How do you create such a subfunction without seeming like creating a function?

■ **Note** This is just one of the scenarios. There may be other situations where such a subfunction (sort of) may be useful for a purpose very different from debugging.

Solution

One very handy answer for such scenarios is associating the function with a block and calling the **subfunction action** (This is not the official term. I am using it here for illustrative purposes. The official term is **block**.) wherever required within the original function (even at multiple places), using the keyword yield.

Such a function can be defined as follows.

```
def check1
        puts "beginning"
        yield
        puts "end"
end
```

This yield signifies a call to a block (executing a code chunk of the block) *that is associated with this function* at that point in the function.

When you call the function, you have to pass the block in such a way that the beginning of the block (either the keyword do, or the {) should start on the same line as the function name (any extra arguments should come before the block).

So the following code is valid.

```
def check1
        puts "beginning"
        yield
        puts "end"
end
puts 'outside the function'
check1 do
    puts 'ok'
end
```

It produces the following.

```
outside the function
beginning
ok
end
```

The last part could have been written like this:

```
check1 {
    puts 'ok'
}
```

Or like this:

```
check1 do puts 'ok' end
```

Or like this:

```
check1 { puts 'ok' }
```

And it would still work well.
But the following won't work.

```
check1
do
        puts 'ok'
end
```

Note that the function could have been defined with a signature involving a reference to a block, like this:

```
def check1(&block)
```

It should work in the same way as the original function when properly invoked.

This is because, even for the original function, the block was working as an implicit argument. *A method doesn't need to specify the block in its signature in order to receive a block parameter.*

Note that if you wish to explicitly define the &block argument, it should come at the end (after other arguments, if any) in the signature.

The following is an example of a function that takes an argument and also uses a block.

```
def check2(name)
        puts "processing #{name}"
        yield
        puts "end"
end
puts 'outside the function'
check2 ('abcd') {
    puts "Hello"
}
```

When run, it should produce the following.

```
outside the function
processing abcd
Hello
end
```

In this sense, a block can be thought of as simply a chunk of code and yield allows you to inject that code at some place in a method.

5.2 Adding Arguments to a Block

Problem

You want to pass arguments to a block to make your code extra efficient.

Solution

Blocks can have their own arguments. (It can be used very effectively to write small and succinct code, which nevertheless can accomplish a great deal). The following is an example.

```
def check3(id)
        puts "processing empid #{id}"
        yield 'Nadia'
        puts "end"
end
puts 'outside the function'
check3 (2) do |str|
   puts "Hello #{str}"
end
```

When run, it should produce the following.

```
outside the function
processing empid 2
Hello Nadia
end
```

Note that id is an argument to the function, but str is an argument to the block; the arguments are separate, and it is possible to have a block with argument and a function that does not take an **explicit** argument). I mention *explicit* argument because the block itself is an implicit argument to the function.

Note that the construct is { | arg1, arg2, ...| <code body of block> }. do-end *can be used* in *place of* {}, *and the block can span multiple lines.*

An example of a multi-argument block is as follows.

```
def multipl
        yield 3,4
end
multipl { |a,b| puts a * b }
```

It should produce this:

```
12
```

The preceding code can be written slightly differently to use a return value.

```
def multipl
        value = yield 3,4
        puts "value is " + value.to_s
end
multipl { |a,b| a * b }
```

And it will produce this:

```
value is 12
```

This is a demonstration of how a block can return a value (the return value from the last statement executed), which may be used in the associated function.

5.3 Initializing and Finalizing Code

Problem

How do you initialize variables for the whole program or execute initializing/finalizing code in Ruby?

Solution

You might have seen the use of these already in an earlier discussion (in context of language elements). But since this is related to a block feature, it is elaborated here in a little more detail.

Every Ruby source file can declare blocks of code to be run as the file is being loaded (the BEGIN blocks) and after the program has finished executing (the END blocks). They are in the following form.

```
BEGIN {
  begin code
}

END {
  end code
}
```

A program may include multiple BEGIN and END blocks. BEGIN blocks are executed in the order they are encountered. END blocks are executed in reverse order.

As an example, the following code

```
BEGIN { x = 'a' ; puts x }
BEGIN { y = 'b' ; puts y }
puts 'general code'
END { a = 'x'; puts a }
END { b = 'y'; puts b }
```

produces this:

```
a
b
general code
y
x
```

This was a demonstration of the order of execution. However, the real use case of such blocks are less dramatic (and possibly more useful).

Imagine that you are working with a lot of CSV files. Very likely, you will get down to splitting strings using a comma as the separator in a lot of places in your code. In such a case, it may save you much hassle (and typing) if you set a default separator for split in the BEGIN block for the entire code, as follows.

```
BEGIN { $; = ',' }
```

And then, use the split function on strings, without mentioning the separator explicitly.

```
line.split #instead of line.split(',')
```

5.4 Iterating over Data

Problem

You need to perform operations on each item in a collection (e.g., each item in an array needs to be multiplied by 2). This may be done by using a for loop and accepting each element of the array, one by one, doing the operation, and possibly putting the result back into the array again (or putting it in another array for the result—and this array needs to be created first). As far as coding goes, it would be easier if there was a simpler method or program construct where you just mention (a) which array to work on and (b) which operation to perform on the elements of the array.

There are other operations that require the collection in its entirety for the operation, but individual elements still participate; for example, sorting the elements of an array based on their values (where individual elements may need comparison with one another in some form). Again, a more traditional solution would require a bit of coding (and the associated debugging, as required). Since sorting is a fairly common operation, it would be nice if a construct existed whereby you specify the array and the operation (sort in this case) and things are done for you.

Ruby provides a lot of iterators that address this scenario perfectly.

Solution

Iterators are essentially methods that execute a block of code multiple times. They are usually used with collections, to perform some function, taking each element of the collection as argument in turn.

Some iterators can also work with ranges. **Ranges can be considered a sequence. For instance, the range 0..9 includes the numbers 0,1,2,3,4,5,6,7,8,9. An iterator can iterate through these numbers, in turn, and perform some action/check using each of them as an argument.**

Some iterators are discussed next.

each

Each is an iterator that works with a range, as well as collections like arrays, hashes, or sets. 'each' (like any other iterator) takes a block as a parameter. The block itself takes a parameter and performs the action specified in the code body of the block, following that

109

parameter. The block parameter gets the value of each of the elements of the collection, in turn. (That is how iterators are designed: the block of the iterator gets passed the collection elements, in turn). In a range, instead of collection elements, it is the numbers (or other things, if it is a non-number range) in the sequence that gets passed in turn.

It's time for an example.

The following code is supposed to take the numbers 1,2,3,4 and 5 in turn and print the square of each of the numbers (followed by a new line).

```
(1..5).each {|i| puts i * i}
```

And so it does.

```
1
4
9
16
25
```

It works very similarly for a set.

```
require 'set'
Set['a','b','c'].each{|x| puts x}
```

That produces this:

```
a
b
c
```

A set has a 'reverse_each' iterator that traverses elements in reverse occurrence order. This is an example of its usage:

```
Set[1,2].reverse_each{ |i| puts i * 2}
```

It should produce the following and also return the set.

```
4
2
```

For an array, however, it is a little trickier. It has the each iterator to traverse thorough the elements of the array.

```
[3,2,5].each {|i| puts i * 2}
```

And that produces the following.

```
6
4
10
```

110

But it also has a few other variations. One is 'each_index' (not applicable to sets or hashes), which is used to traverse through the indexes.

The following code

```
[3,2,5].each_index {|i| print i, ","}
```

produces this:

```
0,1,2,
```

(Note that here print is used with two arguments of different types.)

Another is 'reverse_each', which traverses the elements in the opposite order. Hence, the following

```
[3,2,5].reverse_each {|i| puts i * 2}
```

should produce this:

```
10
4
6
```

For a hash, it gets even better (in the sense that it has more variations of each). There is 'each', 'each_pair' (a synonym for 'each'), 'each_key', 'each_value', and 'reverse_each'. Note the following run in irb (for the hash { 'a' => 100, 'b' => 200 }).

```
irb(main):001:0> h = { 'a' => 100, 'b' => 200 }
=> {"a"=>100, "b"=>200}
irb(main):002:0> h.each {|key, value| puts "key #{key} has value #{value}" }
key a has value 100
key b has value 200
=> {"a"=>100, "b"=>200}
irb(main):003:0> h.each_key {|key| puts key }
a
b
=> {"a"=>100, "b"=>200}
irb(main):004:0> h.each_value {|value| puts value }
100
200
=> {"a"=>100, "b"=>200}
```

'each' here takes two arguments, which gets the key and value for each hash pair. The name of the arguments does not matter. (You could use |k, v| for instances). The first argument gets the key and the second argument gets the value.

It is simpler for 'each_key' and 'each_value'. They work with only one argument.

'reverse_each' works in occurrence order.

```
{1 => 'a', 2=> 'b'}.reverse_each{|k,v| puts k * 2}
```

That produces the following.

```
4
2
```

step

This is an iterator, which is particularly applicable to range, and not to collections.

As you have seen, each (for range) takes one item from the sequence in turn. For an integer sequence like 0..9, it would take, 0,1,2, and so on. However, there may be a case where we do not need each item, but alternate ones. Step can be useful in such situations.

The following code

```
(0..9).step(2){|i| puts "even number : #{i}"}
```

produces this:

```
even number : 0
even number : 2
even number : 4
even number : 6
even number : 8
```

Step could also be more than 2. Note that it can work with non-numeric ranges also.

```
('a'..'e').step(2){|i| puts "letter : #{i}"}
```

That should produce the following.

```
letter : a
letter : c
letter : e
```

select and reject

These are also two well-known iterators. 'reject' is the exact opposite of 'select'. 'select' returns a new collection (which may not be of the same type as the original one)—with elements or items—that satisfies the condition given in the block code. 'reject' returns one—with elements or items—that does not satisfy the condition. Both have in place versions ('select!' and 'reject'), but the in place versions are not available for range.

It really is quiet intuitive, when you see them in action. In a range, it returns an array.

The following code

```
digits = 0..9
ret = digits.select {|i| i < 5 }
puts digits
```

runs as follows.

```
irb(main):001:0> digits = 0..9
=> 0..9
irb(main):002:0> ret = digits.select {|i| i < 5 }
=> [0, 1, 2, 3, 4]
irb(main):003:0> puts digits
0..9
=> nil
```

It has selected items that are less than 5, as expected. Note that the original range is intact.

'reject' in this case does just the opposite (i.e., rejects items that are less than 5).

```
irb(main):002:0> ret = digits.reject {|i| i < 5 }
=> [5, 6, 7, 8, 9]
```

For Arrays

For an array (and set and hash), the in place versions are also available.

The following code run demonstrates the 'select' and 'select!' applied to an array.

```
irb(main):001:0> a = [1,2,3,4,5]
=> [1, 2, 3, 4, 5]
irb(main):002:0> b = a.select { |num|  num.even? }
=> [2, 4]
irb(main):003:0> print a
[1, 2, 3, 4, 5]=> nil
irb(main):004:0> c = a.select! { |num|  num.odd? }
=> [1, 3, 5]
irb(main):005:0> print a
[1, 3, 5]=> nil
```

Eventually, 'reject' has the opposite effect of 'select'.

```
irb(main):006:0> [1,2,3,4,5].reject { |i| i.even? }
=> [1, 3, 5]
```

For Hashes

Note that here the block takes two arguments (although both are not always used).

```
irb(main):001:0> h = { 'a' => 100, 'b' => 200, 'c' => 300 }
=> {"a"=>100, "b"=>200, "c"=>300}
irb(main):002:0> h.select {|k,v| k > 'a'}
=> {"b"=>200, "c"=>300}
```

```
irb(main):003:0> h.select {|k,v| v < 200}
=> {"a"=>100}
irb(main):004:0> print h
{"a"=>100, "b"=>200, "c"=>300}=> nil
irb(main):005:0> h.select! {|k,v| k > 'a'}
=> {"b"=>200, "c"=>300}
irb(main):006:0> print h
{"b"=>200, "c"=>300}=> nil
irb(main):007:0> h.reject! {|k,v| v < 300}
=> {"c"=>300}
irb(main):008:0> print h
{"c"=>300}=> nil
```

For Sets

Note that for sets, the non-in-place versions return an array, not a set.

```
iirb(main):001:0> require 'set'
=> true
irb(main):002:0> s1 = Set[1,2,3,4]
=> #<Set: {1, 2, 3, 4}>
irb(main):003:0> s2 = s1.select { |i| i.even? }
=> [2, 4]
irb(main):004:0> p s1
#<Set: {1, 2, 3, 4}>
=> #<Set: {1, 2, 3, 4}>
irb(main):005:0> s3 = s1.reject { |i| i.odd? }
=> [2, 4]
irb(main):006:0> s4 = s1.reject! { |i| i.even? }
=> #<Set: {1, 3}>
irb(main):007:0> p s1
#<Set: {1, 3}>
=> #<Set: {1, 3}>
irb(main):008:0> print s3
[2, 4]=> nil
```

map or collect

'map' and 'collect' are also useful iterators. There are also in place ('map!' or 'collect!') versions. The non-in-place versions return an array, even when applied to a hash or a set. The hash versions take two arguments. The in place version does not apply to a hash.

They apply a certain function (the code body) to each of the elements in turn and return an array, which is a collection of the results.

For Arrays

```
irb(main):001:0> a = [3,4,5]
=> [3, 4, 5]
irb(main):002:0> a.map {|i| i + 2}
=> [5, 6, 7]
irb(main):003:0> a.collect {|i| i + 2}
=> [5, 6, 7]
irb(main):004:0> print a
[3, 4, 5]=> nil
irb(main):005:0> a.map! {|i| i + 2}
=> [5, 6, 7]
irb(main):006:0> print a
[5, 6, 7]=> nil
```

For Sets

Note that the non-in-place version returns an array.

```
irb(main):001:0> require 'set'
=> true
irb(main):002:0> s1 = Set[1,2]
=> #<Set: {1, 2}>
irb(main):003:0> s2 = s1.map {|i| i * 2}
=> [2, 4]
irb(main):004:0> p s1
#<Set: {1, 2}>
=> #<Set: {1, 2}>
irb(main):005:0> s3 = s1.map! {|i| i * 2}
=> #<Set: {2, 4}>
irb(main):006:0> p s1
#<Set: {2, 4}>
=> #<Set: {2, 4}>
```

For Hashes

It takes two arguments, as usual. (Note that it does not have an in place version).

```
irb(main):001:0> h = {'a' => 1, 'b' => 2}
=> {"a"=>1, "b"=>2}
irb(main):002:0> h.map {|k,v| v + 3}
=> [4, 5]
irb(main):003:0> h.collect {|k,v| v + 3}
=> [4, 5]
irb(main):004:0> print h
{"a"=>1, "b"=>2}=> nil
```

delete_if and keep_if

These are also very useful. As the name suggests, delete_if deletes the elements that satisfy the condition in the given code block (keep_if keeps them). Both of them work in place (even though they don't have an '!' at the end).

For Arrays

```
irb(main):001:0> a = [3,4,5,8,9]
=> [3, 4, 5, 8, 9]
irb(main):002:0> a.keep_if {|i| i.even?}
=> [4, 8]
irb(main):003:0> print a
[4, 8]=> nil
irb(main):004:0> a.delete_if {|i| i.even?}
=> []
irb(main):005:0> print a
[]=> nil
```

For Sets

```
irb(main):001:0> require 'set'
=> true
irb(main):002:0> s1 = Set[3,4,5,6,7]
=> #<Set: {3, 4, 5, 6, 7}>
irb(main):003:0> s2 = Set[3,4,5,6,7]
=> #<Set: {3, 4, 5, 6, 7}>
irb(main):004:0> s1.delete_if{|i| i.even?}
=> #<Set: {3, 5, 7}>
irb(main):005:0> s2.keep_if{|i| i.even?}
=> #<Set: {4, 6}>
irb(main):006:0> p s1
#<Set: {3, 5, 7}>
=> #<Set: {3, 5, 7}>
irb(main):007:0> p s2
#<Set: {4, 6}>
=> #<Set: {4, 6}>
```

For Hashes

```
irb(main):001:0> h = { 'a' => 100, 'b' => 200, 'c' => 300 }
=> {"a"=>100, "b"=>200, "c"=>300}
irb(main):002:0> h.delete_if {|k, v| k > 'b' }
=> {"a"=>100, "b"=>200}
irb(main):003:0> h.keep_if {|k, v| v > 100 }
```

```
=> {"b"=>200}
irb(main):004:0> print h
{"b"=>200}=> nil
```

sort

The sort function has an iterator form (i.e., using block). In the block, a sort order can be specified (which may be other than the default sort order). If no block is specified, the default sort order is followed.

```
irb(main):010:0> Set[4,3,5].sort {|a,b| b<=>a}
=> [5, 4, 3]
irb(main):011:0> { 1 => 'a', 3 => 'c', 2 => 'b'}.sort {|a,b| b<=>a}
=> [[3, "c"], [2, "b"], [1, "a"]]
irb(main):012:0> [2,6,4,5].sort {|a,b| b<=>a}
=> [6, 5, 4, 2]
irb(main):013:0> [2,6,4,5].sort
=> [2, 4, 5, 6]
irb(main):014:0> Set[4,3,5].sort
=> [3, 4, 5]
irb(main):015:0> { 1 => 'a', 3 => 'c', 2 => 'b'}.sort
=> [[1, "a"], [2, "b"], [3, "c"]]
```

Note that upon sort, set returns an array and hash returns an array of arrays (the inner arrays being key-value pairs).

This concludes our current discussion on blocks and iterators. Thus far, quite a few topics have been covered, which (collectively) can be used to tackle some serious programming tasks. You may wish to try your hand at the exercises offered next.

Exercises

The solutions are in the appendix.

Exercise 5.1

You are given a hash in which the key is a student's name and the value is the student's total marks in an exam. Suppose anyone receiving more than 599 (i.e., 600 or more) is placed in the first division. Write a program to print the name and the marks of each student, in a nicely formatted manner, and include 'First Division' in the result if he/she achieved first division.

```
e.g given {"Abani Sen" => 650, "Dora Pridle" => 573}
```

It should print something like this:

```
Abani Sen : Marks obtained 650 : First Division
Dora Pridle : Marks obtained 573
```

Use at least one iterator in the solution.

Exercise 5.2

You are given the following hash.

```
h = {
    "Abani Sen" => 650,
    "Dora Pridle" => 573,
    "Sana Chowdhury" => 824,
    "Pritish Panda" => 732
    }
```

Print the name and marks, sorted by marks, with highest marks at the top.

Exercise 5.3

For entry into engineering or medicine, when the score is calculated, some of the credit is taken from the marks in the exam discussed earlier. These are the rules:

- up to 500 marks: no credit toward entrance

- 501 to 600: 10 credits

- 601 to 700: 20 credits

- 701 to 800: 40 credits

- 801 onward: 70 credits

Write a program to determine and print the credits each of the students received (based on the hash in Exercise 5.2).

CHAPTER 6

■ ■ ■

Input-Output

A lot of the basics have been covered. This should be a good foundation for accomplishing a good variety of programming tasks. Some more bits and pieces will be covered as we go along, but it is good to get down to some tasks and case studies to see the language in action.

The first task discussed (based on a fictitious scenario) is about querying a CSV file, with personal data, for information of interest.

6.1 Querying a CSV File

Problem

Imagine a situation like this. Your company has an elaborate payroll and HR system. However, your department's HR director keeps her own text file with a few details (such as names, birthdays, and so on). She keeps this for somewhat unofficial occasions, like buying a cake for someone's birthday in the department, which is not an enterprise-wide (but departmental and that too somewhat unofficial) event. Suppose it is a generally accepted practice in some other departments too.

The department HR director comes to you, having heard that you are the somewhat recognized expert in manipulating text files (with Ruby scripting), and asks you for help.

The file in question has the following data.

```
Robin,Sen,20/11/1965,360 Karin Drive NSW 2322
Karina,Rhea,23/05/1982, 3/25 West Avenue NSW 2455
Marvin,Major,08/12/1967,210 Racheal Place Vic 3222
John,Doe,15/12/1968,210 Racheal Place Vic 3222
Roland,Boyd,19/02/1992,21 Palm Avenue TAS 5525
```

The birth dates are in dd/mm/yyyy format. The task she wants you to perform (actually a number of subtasks), consists of the following.

- Write a Ruby program to find out a person's birthday, given the first name and the last name as arguments.

- Write a Ruby program to find the youngest person and the oldest person in the department (from the file, of course).

© Malay Mandal 2016
M. Mandal, *Ruby Recipes*, DOI 10.1007/978-1-4842-2469-4_6

- Write a Ruby program to find out the names of all the people with birthdays in a given month (say, December). She is willing to pass the argument as a numeric value (such as 12 for December), rather than as a string, to make your task easier.

She also mentioned that she is not very good at running computer programs, and sometimes she forgets to provide the right arguments while running a program. She does not want to be surprised with a lengthy and/or unintelligible error message. (Those error messages are more for developers). The same is true for a name that she might have misspelled and for which the birthday is not found in the file.

You may argue that for such a small file, someone could just open and read it. But consider that the file could have been considerably bigger. (This is, after all, just a learning exercise. Real-life problems could indeed be larger in scale.) Besides, you may not want to argue with a nice person on such points. She may have come to you because she rather likes you. Also, it may be half a day's worth of work for you and your manager knows about it, so no trouble that way.

Solution

Let's go into each subtask.

Subtask 1: A Person's Birthday

This (sub)task can be further broken down to do the following.

1. Get the arguments: first and last names.

2. Check the argument count. You could do other checks, such as whether it starts with a letter or not, but for now, let's restrict the validation check to the number of arguments only.

3. Find and print out the person's date of birth.

4. Display a nice message when the name is not found.

5. Print out a nice error message when the file is not found in the directory. (She might try to run it from another directory, for instance).

Sound good?

Command-line arguments and ARGV arrays were discussed in Recipe 2.5. They come in handy for argument getting and checking.

Writing the Code

The following code works fine and part of it may be used for argument (getting and) checking.

```
if ARGV.length != 2
        puts "please provide first_name and last_name"
        exit
end
first_name = ARGV[0]
last_name = ARGV[1]
puts "Getting birthday for #{first_name} #{last_name}"
```

Note that the arguments to the program should be separated by a space not a comma. Note also the use of exit for exiting the program midway.

Run the program like this:

```
ruby getnames.rb John Doe
```

You get the following output.

```
Getting birthday for John Doe
```

Omit the last argument, however, and you get the following message.

```
Please provide first_name and last_name
```

Splitting a string based on a particular separator (e.g., ',') has been discussed. To get the date of birth, the third column is needed, while the first and second columns are given as arguments. To get the birthday (including file opening and some error checks), let's first try a hard-coded name. The planned approach is to code it partly and then combine as required.

The following code does the job.

```
first_name = "John"
last_name = "Doe"

begin
        infile = File.open('hrfile.txt','r')
        found = false
        while line = infile.gets
                col = line.split(',')
                #if first and second columns match with the names
                if col[0] == first_name && col[1] == last_name
                        #print date of birth
                        puts "Date of Birth for #{first_name} #{last_name}
                        is #{col[2]}"
                        #mark as found and break
                        found = true
                        break
                end
        end
```

121

```
            #at this point found false means no line has matched the names
            if not found
                    puts "Sorry birthday for #{first_name} #{last_name} not
                    found - check spelling"
            end

rescue
            puts "Could not find file hrfile.txt - check the directory."
ensure
            infile.close unless infile.nil?
end
```

Hard-coded first names and last names do not need arguments to run. This is a way of developing part of a program as full, runnable code, which can later be converted, without much ado, to a function. (This "fast tracks" things a bit so that attention can be focused on other parts of the task). It has a rescue portion, which prints a message if the input file is not found in the directory (*although since this is a general rescue, any other error in its scope will also provide the same error message*). The ensure part closes the file, unless the handler is nil.

Within the while loop, each line picked up is split based on a comma. The first and second columns are attempted for match with the given first_name and last_name, respectively. If a match is found (that means the person's record has been found), the third column (which is the date of birth) is printed, a boolean is marked true, and the while loop is exited with a break. There is no need to read another line if the match is already found.

On the other hand, if all the lines are exhausted and the match is still not found, then an error message is printed, indicating the same (with a slight hint that the spelling may be wrong).

Testing

Objective of testing is used to check that a program is working per its intended purpose. In very general terms, the intended purpose of a program has two main categories.

- It should run successfully when all the settings and arguments are proper (valid case(s).)

- It should fail (with proper error messages, as desirable) when the conditions/arguments are not right (invalid cases(s)). In a good program, the result (output message, etc.) of an invalid case should be indicative of what has gone wrong. (The detail and accuracy of the message indicating the exact error depends on how far the development has gone in tracking the classes of errors accurately.)

In this case, the success objective is (given the file hrfile.txt exists in the same directory, with proper input data as shown earlier) that the program should run as it stands and give John Doe's birthday as '15/12/1968' (from the file). And it does not disappoint. It produces the following.

```
Date of Birth for John Doe is 15/12/1968
```

For error cases in our testing, one very important check makes sure that if the input data file is not present, then this is indicated.

The other check makes sure that if a name is not present in the file, a meaningful message should display to indicate that the name was not found.

For both of these (invalid) cases, the testing requires a bit of tweaking. In the absence of a file, rename the data file to something else (say, hrfile1.txt) and run the code. The output should be as follows.

```
Could not find file hrfile.txt - check the directory.
```

And for the second case, the code itself could be changed (but rename the data file back to its original name). Change the hard-coded first name to "Joe" from "John". (You could say that technically the same is not code being tested if part of the code is changed, and I would agree. However, considering that we are not interested in the hard-coded names in the code, and that the rest of the processing is more important for the final deliverable, it is still a test worth considering).

With "Joe" as the first name, the code should produce the following.

```
Sorry birthday for Joe Doe not found - check spelling
```

It appears that the result is satisfactory.

Appropriately combining this code with the earlier getting and checking arguments (making small additions/deletions/modification as required in the process), the following code is reached.

```
if ARGV.length != 2
        puts "Please provide first_name and last_name"
        exit
end
first_name = ARGV[0]
last_name = ARGV[1]

begin
        infile = File.open('hrfile.txt','r')
        found = false
        while line = infile.gets
                col = line.split(',')
                #if first and second columns match with the names
                if col[0] == first_name && col[1] == last_name
                        #print date of birth
                        puts "Date of Birth for #{first_name} #{last_name}
                        is #{col[2]}"
```

```
                            #mark as found and break
                            found = true
                            break
                   end
           end
           #at this point found false means no line has matched the names
           if not found
                   puts "Sorry birthday for #{first_name} #{last_name} not
                   found - check spelling"
           end

rescue
           puts "Could not find file hrfile.txt - check the directory."
ensure
           infile.close unless infile.nil?
end
```

And, it works well.

Subtask 2: (The Names of) the Youngest and the Oldest Persons

This (sub)task does not require getting any argument to the program. It works on all the rows. This can be broken down to three parts.

1. Get the third column.

2. Change it into yyyymmdd format (this will make it easy to compare numerically).

3. Sort the yyyymmdd values to get the minimum and the maximum. Store the corresponding names.

Again, you can take a build by portions approach.

Getting the third column is simple. But for the later part of the code, it is better if we get the first name and last name along with that (because eventually we have to print the names of the youngest and the oldest persons, not their dates of birth).

With the rescue and ensure parts tagged on, the code looks like this:

```
begin
           infile = File.open('hrfile.txt','r')
           while line = infile.gets
                   col = line.split(',')
                   puts "#{col[0]} #{col[1]} #{col[2]}"
           end
rescue
           puts "Could not find file hrfile.txt - check the directory."
ensure
           infile.close unless infile.nil?
end
```

(This should require no explanation at this point). The output is as follows.

```
Robin Sen 20/11/1965
Karina Rhea 23/05/1982
Marvin Major 08/12/1967
John Doe 15/12/1968
Roland Boyd 19/02/1992
```

You somehow need to have the date format changed to yyyymmdd. For this purpose, again, you can resort to writing a small code with a hard-coded value.

The following code does not disappoint you.

```
orgdate = "20/11/1965"
dtpart = orgdate.split('/')
print "#{dtpart[2]}#{dtpart[1]}#{dtpart[0]}"
```

It prints the date converted in that format. It should output as follows **(in this case without adding a newline at the end of output, as print is being used).**

```
19651120
```

Finally, for the sorting (you actually need to do two types sorting: one for the minimum and one for the maximum), you use another piece of code, which works on a smaller data file (named input2.txt and having data as shown here).

```
Robin Sen 19651120
Karina Rhea 19820523
Marvin Major 19671208
```

The following code seems to work.

```
mindate = 30000000; maxdate = 1

infile = File.new('input2.txt','r')
while (line = infile.gets)
        col = line.chomp.split
        date = col[2].to_i
        if (mindate > date)
                mindate = date
                oldest = "#{col[0]} #{col[1]}"
        end
        if (maxdate < date)
                maxdate = date
                youngest = "#{col[0]} #{col[1]}"
        end
end
infile.close
```

```
puts "Youngest : #{youngest}"
puts "Oldest : #{oldest}"
```

When run, it should produce this:

```
Youngest : Karina Rhea
Oldest : Robin Sen
```

Note that mindate is set at a rather high value (higher than you should expect in the data set) and maxdate is set at a rather low value, to start with. This is to ensure that the very first comparison finds a new minimum value (or a new maximum value, as the case may be); otherwise, the algorithm may not work properly.

For any one comparison, if the date needs switching (a new candidate date is found), the designated (oldest or youngest) name is reassigned too (to the value from the corresponding row). After all the rows are processed, it is left with the names of the youngest and the oldest persons.

Since the whole solution is being built in a piecewise fashion, this part of the program uses an intermediate data format (in a limited quantity) to develop the processing logic.

Putting it all together (and doing some amendments), the final code, which reads from the actual data file, looks like this:

```
mindate = 30000000; maxdate = 1

begin
        #open input file
        infile = File.open('hrfile.txt','r')

        #read and process lines in a loop
        while line = infile.gets
                #split line for individual columns
                col = line.split(',')

                #split date for individual date parts
                dtpart = col[2].split('/')

                #reassemble date parts in yyyymmdd format for easy sorting
                date = "#{dtpart[2]}#{dtpart[1]}#{dtpart[0]}".to_i

                #check if it is a new minimum
                if (mindate > date)
                        mindate = date
                        oldest = "#{col[0]} #{col[1]}"
                end
```

```
            #check if it is a new maximum
            if (maxdate < date)
                    maxdate = date
                    youngest = "#{col[0]} #{col[1]}"
            end
        end
    rescue
        puts "Could not find file input.txt - check the directory."
    ensure
        infile.close unless infile.nil?
    end

#print the result(s)
puts "Youngest : #{youngest}"
puts "Oldest : #{oldest}"
```

Note that this code may be further optimized, but it shows a generalist approach to solving a problem. For instance, the checks for maximum and minimum could have been done within an if-else structure, rather than using two if statements. (After all, the same date is unlikely to be both the maximum and the minimum.) As another example, the date formatting could have been handled using a proper API.

Date Handling by API

Ruby has a Date class that has an elaborate API for parsing, formatting, and otherwise using dates. You need to require the file to use them.

Here is a small example to show the parsing and formatting of dates. Using these, you could process the date for this task.

The following code

```
require 'date'
dt = Date.parse('3/2/1965')
puts dt.strftime('%Y%m%d')
```

should produce this:

```
19650203
```

It is possible to provide the parse format explicitly, for example:

```
dt = Date.parse('03/02/1965','%d/%m/%Y')
```

Sometimes it may be necessary.

Subtask 3: Persons with a Birthday in a Given Month

This one is quite simple. Broadly, the steps are as follows.

1. Check that the first argument (integer value) is between 1 and 12 (both ends included).

2. Add 0 to the front if the integer is less than 10.

3. Compare it with the middle part (as split by '/') of the third column (as split by ','), and if a match is found, print the name.

(Note that this is also done without using the Date API).
The following is the code, detailed properly.

```ruby
if ARGV.length < 1
        puts "Please provide the month [1 to 12]"
        exit
end

month1 = ARGV[0].to_i #Dec will become 0
if month1 < 1 or month1 > 12
        puts "Wrong format or month number : valid 1 to 12"
        exit
end

if month1 < 10
        month = "0" + month1.to_s
else
        month = month1.to_s
end

begin
        infile = File.open('hrfile.txt','r')

        found = false
        while line = infile.gets
                col = line.split(',')
                birthmonth = col[2].split('/')[1]
                if birthmonth.eql?(month)
                        puts "#{col[0]} #{col[1]}"
                        found = true
                end
        end
rescue
        puts "Could not find file hrfile.txt - check the directory."
ensure
        infile.close unless infile.nil?
end

puts "No record found for given month" if not found
```

The following are some of the main test cases for this:

- Provide no argument.

- Provide a string as an argument, such as Dec.

- Provide a valid two-digit month (such as 12) that should fetch record(s).

- Provide a valid single-digit month that should fetch a record.

- Provide a month number (such as 1) that should not fetch any record.

With no argument, this is the output:

```
Please provide the month [1 to 12]
```

With Dec as the argument, this is the output:

```
Wrong format or month number : valid 1 to 12
```

With 12 as the argument, this is the output:

```
Marvin Major
John Doe
```

With 5 as the argument, this is the output:

```
Karina Rhea
```

And with 1 as the argument (it does not have a corresponding record in the data file), this is the output:

```
No record found for given month
```

Note that if you provide more than one argument, the second argument onward is ignored. (No check is in place for argument count). Also, initially, the first argument is converted to int (actually Fixnum). This makes comparison easier.

Now you can confidently deliver the programs to the department HR director (if the situation was not fictitious, that is).

6.2 Sorting Text

Problem

The next task demonstrates taking user input (from a console) in a loop and processing the data once the end of the input is signaled. So you want to take names, one by one in a loop, from the command prompt, unless the user enters the string END. Then, sort those names in alphabetical order and print them out.

Solution

The following code will work.

```
print "Name [enter END to end] : "

name_arr = []

while name = gets.chomp
  case name
  when "END"
    puts "No more input signalled by user"
    break # break from asking loop
  else # some name
       #append the name to the array
       name_arr << name
       #print the prompt again for further input
       print "Name [enter END to end] : "
  end
end

#sort the array and print the result
name_arr.sort.each {|name| puts name}
```

When run, this code should keep printing the prompt and wait for the user to input a name (one at a time). Once the input is END (all uppercase), it stops asking for input and provides the output (i.e., prints a sorted list of the names—one per line, as expected from puts function).

Here is an example.

```
=>ruby arngname1.rb
Name [enter END to end] : John
Name [enter END to end] : Jane
Name [enter END to end] : Dora
Name [enter END to end] : Tully
Name [enter END to end] : Peter
Name [enter END to end] : END
No more input signalled by user
Dora
Jane
John
Peter
Tully
```

How It Works

The code has a lot of comments and it would be helpful to follow them. But as you can see, it is essentially using a while loop to get the names one by one, and using chomp to remove the newline characters following the names (because the user is supposed to press the Enter key every time after entering the name). It also has a conditional break in case END is entered instead of a name.

A print for prompt is required before the while in order to prompt for the first name, because the while condition has a gets call (where it would stop without giving any decent clue to the user that it is waiting for a name).

Once the names are all taken, the real work happens in one line of code (sorting and printing). This is where Ruby shines (over Java for instance) in this kind of quick scripting.

6.3 Checking User Input

Problem

Let's continue with the problem from Recipe 6.2, except a name list should be sorted by last name. (Make sure that you read the previous recipe before continuing with this recipe.)

Since we are taking input from user, there may be a check for proper names (for now let's define a proper name as any name that does not have a digit in it). Also, what if someone inadvertently enters the first name and then presses the Return key (without entering the last name)? We can check for that too (reject it, but show the proper message in the next prompt, so that the user notices).

How about enhancing the last solution with all of these checks? Note that different parts of the name should be separated in the input by one or more spaces. And the names should be printed with the last name first and then rest of the name (e.g., "John M McCain" => McCain John M).

Solution

Before fully addressing the solution, I would like to present a bit of *regex* (or regular expressions). Although regular expressions are discussed in detail later in the book, for the current exercise a bit of discussion is necessary.

Note that a representation like /[0-9]/, when used as a pattern (to be matched or searched for), means any character (strictly speaking, any one character) that is between 0 and 9. It can be searched in a string for a match (or otherwise) with the =~ operator (which you would have already seen).

For instance, this:

```
"ab11ed" =~ /[0-9]/
```

returns this:

2

It is the first index position of a digit (any digit, or any character between 0 and 9, both included) in the string. However, **if the string does not have any digit, it returns nil, (which, as you might remember, is interpreted as 'false' in a logical context**).

These kinds of expressions (e.g., [0-9]) are known as *regular expressions* (there are many forms possible). Encased between / and /, it forms a regex pattern (/ and / denote pattern boundaries in this case). Note that a pattern can be an exact string (like /ab/) also.

Equipped with that knowledge, let's proceed to the solution. Since we already have some code in place from Recipe 6.2, it would be a good idea to solve the missing pieces first. We also already have the non-digit check in place.

In order to check that the name given has at least the first name and the last name, we can split it in one or more spaces (again a regular expression). The resulting array from split has at least size 2; something like this:

```
names = name.split(/\s+/)
names.size > 1
```

The first line of code splits a string (named name) based on the regular expression \s+ (\s indicates whitespace characters and the + indicates one or more of that). The result of the split goes into the names array. The next line checks whether the size of the array is greater than 1.

The next piece of the puzzle is to get the last name and the rest of the names. (Note that the name may or may not have a middle name, so the array size after the split will not always be 2).

We could find the array size and then access the last element of the array based on the size. The following is an example.

```
a = ['John','M','McCain']
i = a.size
lastName = a[i-1]
```

Note that there is a function named last in the Array API that gives the last element of an array.

```
irb(main):004:0> ['John','M','McCain'].last
=> "McCain"
```

But we need to do more than that. We need to rearrange the name (with last_name coming at the beginning). An approach for index lookup based on size (i.e. lastName = a[i-1]) is more suitable.

In terms of conceptual design, the solution has three main *functional components*.

- Reading and validating the name (and converting valid names to bring the last name first).

- Asking for names in a loop, until END, and building up the name array for sorting.

- Sorting and printing.

Note the following.

- The functional components do not necessarily represent the sequential part of the code. It represents breaking up overall processing into some main basic chunk of activities. Those activities or functionalities may be intertwined in the program and they may not necessarily come one after another. (For instance, validation should be called as part of a looping action, as each name needs to be validated).

- Note also that the first component (as stated earlier) could be broken down into subfunctions. For example, validating the name and transforming a valid name could be two separate functions. It could be a matter of design choice (and indeed another function may be written, which could be passed a valid name for transformation), but the transformation part is rather small, so in terms of design, I have put it in the same function as the validation.

Now let's come back to solving individual functions (three of them), from our conceptual functional component model.

The third part (sorting and printing), in essence, is same as the last task. Hence, more or less the same code may be used.

For the second part, we now have three essential cases.

- END: To signal the end of looping

- A valid (and converted) name => add to the name_array

- An invalid name => ask again, and signal error to user through the same message

This means that our case statement has three cases now—one for each class of action in the while loop. It would be good if our validation function supports this classification (so that the case statement can work directly on the output of the function, and need not have anything to do with the raw name).

The following is the classification functionality to implement.

- Return END when that string is specified.

- Return a specific string that indicates that the name is invalid (and also indicates the type of error in the same output string—meaning that we may have more than one specific error string)

- Return the converted name (last name first) for all other (i.e., valid) cases.

You can start implementing from the first functionality, which is this classification. The following code should work fine.

```ruby
def validate(name)
        if name == "END"
                "END"
        elsif name =~ /[0-9]/
                "NOTVALID_NUMERIC"
```

```
        else
                names = name.split(/\s+/)
                sz = names.size
                if sz < 2
                        "NOTVALID_FIRSTNAMEONLY"
                else #return the name with last part first
                        last_name = names.delete_at(sz-1)
                        names.insert(0,last_name)
                        names.join(' ')
                end
        end
end

puts validate('John M McCain')
puts validate('END')
puts validate('FirstNameOnly')
puts validate('1abc 2def')
puts validate('123NumericAndFirstNameOnly')
```

When run, it should produce the following.

```
McCain John M
END
NOTVALID_FIRSTNAMEONLY
NOTVALID_NUMERIC
NOTVALID_NUMERIC
```

Note that the function first checks for digits and then the first name only. Hence, a case containing both issues is reported as a numeric case. (Note also that many of the code features used in the function were discussed prior to this solution).

Equipped with this function, the case part can be written without much trouble. The while loop (including the case statement) now becomes this:

```
while name = gets.chomp
  processed_name = validate(name)
  case processed_name
  when "END"
    puts "end of user input"
    break # break from asking loop
  when "NOTVALID_NUMERIC"
        print "Not a valid name (no digit allowed). Name [enter END to end] : "
  when "NOTVALID_FIRSTNAMEONLY"
        print "Please provide full name. Name [enter END to end] : "
  else # valid (and converted) name
        #append the name to the array
        name_arr << processed_name
```

```
        #print the prompt again for further input
        print "Name [enter END to end] : "
  end
end
```

Two different types of error messages have been provided, so there are two cases for that, but those two cases could be merged if you want to provide one general error message. Those two cases are functionally not very different.

This is the current solution.

```
<function definition goes here>

print "Name [enter END to end] : "
name_arr = []

<while loop goes here>

puts
puts "--------------------------"
puts "Sorted names (by last name)"
puts "--------------------------"
#sort the array and print the result
name_arr.sort.each {|name| puts name}
```

Run with the inputs demonstrated next.

```
Name [enter END to end] : 123
Not a valid name (no digit allowed). Name [enter END to end] : abcd
Please provide full name. Name [enter END to end] : Tori Dean
Name [enter END to end] : John M McCain
Name [enter END to end] : Daly Moore
Name [enter END to end] : Santu Bose
Name [enter END to end] : David Bower
Name [enter END to end] : END
end of user input
```

It produces the following.

```
--------------------------
Sorted names (by last name)
--------------------------
Bose Santu
Bower David
Dean Tori
McCain John M
Moore Daly
```

This satisfies our specification.

6.4 Storing Data in a Structured Manner

Problem

Sometimes we need to store data in a structured manner, access and change (or otherwise process) them as part of the structure, and provide the necessary output. It may be more convenient (or conceptually easier to reason about/or easier to maintain) data in a structured format that represents an entity in the business domain.

Solution

In this situation, a struct can be very helpful. Struct is a class that makes it easy to organize and handle data.

Suppose we need to keep our customers' names, addresses, and telephone numbers to do various processing. It would be nice if, for each customer, we could group this information together (with possibly a short name [actually a variable] that identifies each customer for later retrieval and/or processing of his/her information).

We can do this in the following ways:

```
Struct.new("Customer", :name, :addr, :tel)
```

or

```
Customer = Struct.new(:name, :addr, :tel)
```

Either way creates a structure named Customer, which has the structure described (i.e., three fields named name, addr, and tel—in that order).

And multiple customer data can be created using the structure, as follows.

```
john = Customer.new("John Connor", "123 Rachel Close", 3456)
jane = Customer.new("Jane Greystoke", "12 Jungle House", 4568)
turno = Customer.new("Sarah Turnbull", "50 Sunset Boulevard", 1254)
```

The variables (john, jane, etc.) can then be used to access particular data in those structures. Here is an example.

```
irb(main):005:0> john.name
=> "John Connor"
irb(main):006:0> jane.tel
=> 4568
```

It can even be changed by assigning a new value.

```
irb(main):007:0> jane.tel = 1111
=> 1111
irb(main):008:0> jane.tel
=> 1111
```

It is possible to define a structure with methods also. Check the following code.

```
Customer = Struct.new(:name, :addr, :tel) do
  def greeting
    puts "Hello #{name}!"
  end
end
john = Customer.new("John Connor", "123 Rachel Close", 3456)
john.greeting
```

It does the job nicely, and when run, it should produce this:

```
Hello John Connor!
```

There are multiple ways to access the fields in a struct. For instance, each of the following accesses the name john (and should return "John Connor").

```
john['name']
john[:name]
john[0]
```

One way may be more desirable than others in some situations. It also may be a matter of style, but I would recommend to follow the john.name style, unless some other style is really required for the situation.

Note that it is also possible to very easily use a customer array, which may be iterated through for processing.

The following code

```
Customer = Struct.new(:name, :addr, :tel)

cust = []

cust[0] = Customer.new("John Connor", "123 Rachel Close", 3456)
cust[1] = Customer.new("Jane Greystoke", "12 Jungle House", 4568)
cust[2] = Customer.new("Sarah Turnbull", "50 Sunset Boulevard", 1254)

cust.each { |c| puts c.name }
```

should produce this:

```
John Connor
Jane Greystoke
Sarah Turnbull
```

It is also possible to iterate through each field of a single struct's data. For example, in the preceding structure, if we define another customer like this:

```
joe = Customer.new("Joe Smith", "123 Maple St", 12345)
```

we can iterate through each field of this particular customer data, as follows.

```
joe.each_pair {|name, val| puts("#{name} => #{val}") }
```

It should produce the following.

```
name => Joe Smith
addr => 123 Maple St
tel => 12345
```

There are other methods in the Struct API for various functionalities. For instance, the == or eql? method checks the equality between two structures.

The following code

```
Customer = Struct.new(:name, :addr, :tel)
cust = []
cust[0] = Customer.new("John Connor", "123 Rachel Close", 3456)
joe = Customer.new("Joe Smith", "123 Maple St", 12345)
j2 = Customer.new("John Connor", "123 Rachel Close", 3456)
puts j2 == joe
puts j2 == cust[0]
```

should produce this:

```
false
true
```

This concludes our current discussion on structs.

6.5 Working with Directories

Problem

You want to work with directories in the file system.

Solution

While dealing with tasks at the directory level of a file system, methods in the Dir class may come handy. Objects of this class are directory streams that represent directories in the file system (in a sense like directory handlers).

Using this API, you can create directories, change directories, list files in a directory, and so on without resorting to firing an OS-level command through the Ruby code. What is more, you can work further on the return values. Let's take, for instance, when you list the files using the proper Dir method. Since you have a handle on the list of files, you can iterate through the list, and take some particular action on each file. It can usually work with both relative (from a current directory in execution context) and absolute paths.

■ **Note** The current directory in the execution context may not be the directory from which you fired the script. It is possible that you programmatically changed the directory to a new one (in which case the new directory becomes your current directory in the program execution context).

Some of these functions can work with blocks.

mkdir

The mkdir function creates a directory.

```
Dir.mkdir('test1') => will create a directory 'test1' under the current
working directory.
Dir.mkdir('test2',777) => will create directory 'test2' with '777'
permission.
```

rmdir

The rmdir function removes the named directory, if empty. It raises an error otherwise. It can work with a relative or an absolute path.

```
Dir.rmdir('/tmp/tst')    #absoulte path
Dir.rmdir('test2')       #relative path
```

pwd

The pwd function returns the path to the current directory in the execution context. (It does not print it, it just returns. So you need to use puts or some such function, if you need it printed.)

```
irb(main):001:0> currDir = Dir.pwd
=> "/Users/Shared/chap02"
irb(main):002:0> puts currDir
/Users/Shared/chap02
=> nil
```

chdir

The chdir function changes the directory programmatically. Once changed, the new directory becomes current in an execution context.

```
irb(main):001:0> Dir.chdir('test1')
=> 0
irb(main):002:0> puts Dir.pwd
/Users/Shared/chap06/test1
=> nil
```

chdir has a few forms. Without an argument, it changes to the HOME directory (the HOME variable should be set in the environment). Used with a block, it changes the directory to the named directory, executes the block, and upon exiting from the block, the original working directory (which was current prior to the chdir) is restored in the execution context. The return value of chdir in this case is the return value of the block. (This form should be used carefully in a multithreaded coding.)

The following code

```
puts Dir.pwd
Dir.chdir('test1') {
        puts Dir.pwd
        2 + 2
}
puts Dir.pwd
```

produces this:

```
/Users/Shared/chap06
/Users/Shared/chap06/test1
/Users/Shared/chap06
```

home

Without an argument, the home function returns the home directory of the current user. With an argument, it returns the home directory of the named user.

```
Dir.home => Returns the home directory, of the current user.
Dir.home('root') => Returns roots home directory.
```

exist?

For the given argument, the exist? function checks that it is the name of an existing directory . If it is not a directory or does not exist, either case returns false. (Path specification for relative from current or absolute applies. See the example below.)

```
Dir.exist?('test2') => checks if the directory 'test2' exists directly under
the current directory.
```

entries

The common form of the entries function takes one argument, which is the name of a directory whose entries are required. For a valid argument (directory exists), it returns an array containing the names of all files and directories in that directory. (A non-existing directory as an argument raises an error).

For the current directory, '.' may be passed (dot, surrounded by quotes) as the argument.

```
irb(main):003:0> Dir.entries('.')
=> [".", "..", "test1", "test2"]
irb(main):004:0> Dir.entries('test1')
=> [".", "..", "x.txt", "y.txt"]
```

new

The new function returns a new directory object for the named directory. This can be used as a handle for further action. It can use the close function on this handle (directory stream) to close it after the job is done. (See the next function's example.)

each

The each function works on a directory stream with a block, where the name of each file/ directory from the entries of the directory stream (i.e., the name of files / directories in the directory, which is pointed to by this directory stream or handle) gets passed as an argument.

The following code illustrates the point.

```
dir = Dir.new('test1')
print dir.entries
puts
dir.each {|x| puts 'Got '+ x}
dir.close
```

It can produce something like this:

```
[".", "..", "test3", "x.txt", "y.txt"]
Got .
Got ..
Got test3
Got x.txt
Got y.txt
```

Note that the '.' and '..' are also included in the array.

foreach

The foreach function has many forms, but only one is discussed here. It uses block and works similarly to each. However, instead of explicitly opening the directory stream with Dir.new, here the directory name is passed as an argument (hence, no explicit closing is required). In this sense, it is more convenient than each (less code).

In the test1 example, the following one liner

```
Dir.foreach('test1') {|x| puts "Name :  #{x}"}
```

produces this:

```
Name :  .
Name :  ..
Name :  test3
Name :  x.txt
Name :  y.txt
```

glob

The glob function is, by far, the most useful function in the Dir class, so it is going to be discussed in detail. It essentially filters the files to be worked on (for filtered values, files and directories are the same in the sense that filtering is done on names, and hence, it picks up names or either files or directories in the context), rather than all the entries, and that is very useful sometimes. This is shown in the following examples, as well as in the context of at least one upcoming task.

It can take regular expressions, as patterns, for filtering. As a further goody, you don't have to deal with the '.' and '..'. Some examples are given next.

Dir.glob('')* #returns all files in the current directory (but excludes '.' and '..')

```
irb(main):002:0> Dir.glob('*')
=> ["chdir.rb", "each.rb", "foreach.rb", "test1", "test2"]
```

It is possible to get a list of files with a particular extension (e.g., .rb).

Dir.glob('*.rb') #gets a list of file (and directory) names ending in *.rb* from the current directory.

```
irb(main):004:0> Dir.glob("*.rb")
=> ["chdir.rb", "each.rb", "foreach.rb"]
```

'**' works recursively. So finding any file with the .rb extension in any subdirectory under the current directory can be achieved using Dir.glob('**/*.rb'). Note that the default file separator may vary based on the operating system, so you can use File.join to build up the path, instead of a direct string.

```
irb(main):001:0> path = File.join('**','*.rb')
=> "**/*.rb"
irb(main):002:0> Dir.glob(path) #effectively Dir.glob("**/*.rb") in this case
=> ["chdir.rb", "each.rb", "foreach.rb", "test1/test3/z.rb", "test1/x.rb",
"test1/y.rb"]
```

It is possible to restrict recursive search to any subdirectory with a particular name. For instance, we can get all the .rb files under any test3 directory anywhere (at any sublevel) under the current directory, as follows.

```
irb(main):003:0> Dir.glob('**/test3/*.rb')
=> ["test1/test3/z.rb"]
```

It is also possible to use an expression like '**/test1/**/*.rb', which indicates any .rb file at any sublevel of any directory named test1 (which itself could be at any sublevel under the current directory).

```
irb(main):004:0> Dir.glob('**/test1/**/*.rb')
=> ["test1/test3/z.rb", "test1/x.rb", "test1/y.rb"]
```

Eventually, there are other patterns possible (and a sensible combination of patterns would also work). Any files (or directories) that start with t would be as follows.

```
irb(main):005:0> Dir.glob('t*')
=> ["test1", "test2"]
```

And any file (or directory) that has each in it would be as follows.

```
irb(main):006:0> Dir.glob('*each*')
=> ["each.rb", "foreach.rb"]
```

It is possible to search among multiple extensions. The following code finds all files (or directories) in the current directory, which has either extension .rb or .txt.

```
irb(main):001:0> Dir.glob('*.{rb,txt}')
=> ["chdir.rb", "each.rb", "foreach.rb", "x.txt", "y.txt"]
```

This pattern used a regular expression (for pattern alteration) of the form {p, q}.

It is possible to find files (or directories) that have an extension whose first character is not r (anything but r). Here, a regular expression is used. (The regular expression [^r] means a single character that is anything but r).

```
irb(main):003:0> Dir.glob('*.[^r]*')
=> ["x.txt", "y.txt"]
```

Note that it will not pick up a file (name) that does not have a '.' in its name (thus all files without extensions will be excluded). This is because the overall pattern includes the '.' character, and hence, it looks for the dot in the name of the file (or directory).

6.6 Dividing Files into Subdirectories

Problem

This task is rather simple. There are some files in a directory. All of them have the .sql extension. But some are table creation scripts (these have a 'create table' string in the first line); others are procedure creation scripts (they have the 'create procedure' string in the first line). From the name or extension, it is not distinguishable whether a file has a table creation script or a procedure creation script inside it. Your task is to write a script to do the following.

1. Create two subdirectories (named tbl and proc) in the current directory.

2. Get the .sql files, one by one, and find out whether the first line matches table or procedure.

3. Move the file to the appropriate subfolder.

Solution

To test the program, you need input data (files). Create four files named a.sql, b.sql, c.sql, and d.sql, respectively. In the first two files, put 'create table a' and 'create table b' in the first line (and some text in the second line). Here is an example.

```
create table a
    col  a1   null
```

For the last two files, use 'create procedure' in the first line. Here is an example.

```
create procedure c
    begin
```

If you think about the steps in the task, how to create a directory (the first part) has already been discussed (using the Dir API). How to move a file programmatically (the third part) has not been.

In the second part of the task, given the file name, you could open it, get the first line, and use the match operator to find out if it contains 'table' or 'procedure'. The Dir API can also be used to get only the .sql files in the directory.

To move a file, you can use the mv function of FileUtils. One example is given next. (Note that this is a rather crude example without any exception handling, but it shows the basic code.)

```
require 'fileutils'
FileUtils.mv('abc.txt','tbl')
#FileUtils.mv('abc.txt','tbl/abc.txt')
```

Provided that the abc.txt file exists in the current directory, the second line of the code will rename the file (unless a tbl directory exists under the current directory). The third line (when uncommented) will have a proper move effect (and not rename), provided that the files and directories exist as desired.

To get the names of all the .sql files in the current directory, you can use the following code.

```
arr = Dir.glob('*.sql')
print arr
```

It takes the file names in an array and prints the array.

```
["a.sql", "b.sql", "c.sql", "d.sql"]
```

And the array can be iterated over using block structure and the each method. Putting it altogether, the code looks like this:

```
require 'fileutils'
Dir.mkdir('tbl')
Dir.mkdir('proc')

arr = Dir.glob('*.sql')
arr.each {|filename|
        infile = File.open(filename,'r')
        firstline = infile.gets #just need to read the first line
        infile.close
        FileUtils.mv(filename,'tbl') if firstline =~ /table/
        FileUtils.mv(filename,'proc') if firstline =~ /procedure/
}
```

■ **Note** **Instead of** Dir.mkdir('tbl'), FileUtils.mkdir('tbl') **will also work.**

This is somewhat crude but it works. Since we need only the first line, there is no need to use a while loop on the files. Also, it is very important that the opened file be closed prior to the move.

This was a simple use case. In reality, a file's content may be more complicated (such as the table keyword appearing on the second line, or the word 'procedure' appears first in a table creation script file, within a commented part, not to mention case insensitive keywords). Also, no proper error handling has been added to this code. In a real-life task, unless you are running it yourself and you are able to monitor the run and the results, it is imperative that proper error handling be in place.

Repeated running of the code would create problem because the (sub) directories are already created. To avoid this, you could change the lines for directory creation as follows.

```
Dir.mkdir('tbl') unless File.directory?('tbl')
Dir.mkdir('proc') unless File.directory?('proc')
```

This means that the directory creation for each one would not be attempted if already present.

6.7 Adding Text to Files Using a Batch Operation

Problem

(The following is a fictitious situation. Any resemblance …)

Dale is the team leader of Zoran's team.

Dale stormed into the meeting room.

"Guys, we have a situation."

The team members waited eagerly in anticipation.

"Our team has been chosen to be audited this year."

This was not good news, thought Zoran.

"You know how fussy they are about coding standards. Do those Java files in our project have a header with the project name and the code owner's name?" Dale asked.

Zoran didn't like where this was going. He was the unofficial batch script expert on the team, and he was pretty sure nobody bothered to put those comments in place (he himself didn't).

"Zoran?" Dale looked around to face Zoran as he spoke. "Write a script that can run from the project root directory, identify all the .java files, and add the header as a comment on the first line. Let me know when it is done."

"Who should I put for the code owner's name ?" Zoran asked.

"Use my name for now. My full name." Dale replied.

Solution

For this task, the first thing to do is to identify the (.java) file names in the project, using the full path from the root directory. I will show two ways of achieving it. The second one is really easy for the task, but the first approach may be useful (with some modifications as appropriate) in other situations (as a more general approach).

To test the code, create a set of directories (and subdirectories) under the current directory.

```
a
b/1
```

a and b are the immediate subdirectories. 1 is a subdirectory of b.

In a, create a file called abc.java. In 1, create another file named def.java. Each of the files should have two lines.

```
111
222
```

That is not Java code (far from it). But our aim is to test our script, and this should be fine for our purpose. Finally, these are the subfolders and files of concern (other than the Ruby script itself):

```
a/abc.java
b/1/def.java
```

Approach 1: Output From Command Execution

In Mac or Linux (tested on a Mac), the following command

```
find . -name *.java -print
```

outputs as follows.

```
./a/abc.java
./b/1/def.java
```

You can get the return value of a command, as a single string, with the backquote construct.

```
val = `find . -name *.java -print`
```

The %x () construct also works in the same way. The following code

```
val = %x(find . -name *.java -print)
val.gsub!("\n",'')
puts val
arr = val.split("./")
print arr
```

prints as follows.

```
./a/abc.java./b/1/def.java
["", "a/abc.java", "b/1/def.java"]
```

The first line of the code gets the whole return in a string (val). The second line replaces all the newlines in the string, in place. (Make sure to use double quotes for \n, not single quotes).

The fourth line splits the string based on the ./.

Note that we still need to get rid of the first element of the array. Check the following code.

```
#get return value of command in a string
val = %x(find . -name *.java -print)

#replace all \n characters
val.gsub!("\n",'')

#split by ./ and take the second element onwards
#array of .java filenames with full path starting form current directory
arr = val.split("./")[1..-1]

print arr
```

This code populates the arr array the way that we need.

```
["a/abc.java", "b/1/def.java"]
```

This approach of running an OS-level command, getting the output, and processing may be useful elsewhere.

Approach 2: Use Dir.glob

This one is really easy.

```
arr = Dir.glob('**/*.java')
print arr
```

It prints as follows.

```
["a/abc.java", "b/1/def.java"]
```

Adding the Comments in Each File

Now that you know how to get the file names in an array, let's use the second approach for that. Also suppose that the comment line to be added in each .java file (in the beginning) is as follows.

```
//Project : Silvasa ; code owner : Dale Nordstrom
```

Create a new file (tmp.txt) for writing. Write the comment line (appropriately escaping special characters, if necessary) and then write the whole of the designated file in that. Next, close the file, delete the original one, and rename the tmp.txt file as the original one.

The code looks like this.

```
require 'fileutils'

arr = Dir.glob('**/*.java')
arr.each {|filename|
        outfile = File.open('tmp.txt','w')
        outfile.puts "//Project : Silvasa ; code owner : Dale Nordstrom"
        infile = File.open(filename,'r')
        while line = infile.gets
                outfile.puts line
        end
        infile.close
        outfile.close
        FileUtils.mv('tmp.txt',filename)
}
```

This code works. A slightly shorter approach (which does not process the input files line by line) is illustrated in the following code, which works too.

```
require 'fileutils'

Dir.glob('**/*.java').each {|filename|
        outfile = File.open('tmp.txt','w')
        outfile.puts "//Project : Silvasa ; code owner : Dale Nordstrom"
        outfile.puts(File.read(filename))
        outfile.close
        FileUtils.mv('tmp.txt',filename)
}
```

Note that no protection is built in against multiple runs. Multiple runs in this case create one line of comment per run, which is not very desirable from an auditing point of view.

CHAPTER 7

■ ■ ■

Regular Expressions

A regular expression is a sequence of symbols and characters, expressing a string or a pattern, to be searched for within a longer piece of text.

■ **Note** Support and implementation of regular expressions may vary from language to language. In this chapter, it is discussed in the context of Ruby. However, some prominent regular expression tokens and constructs likely work in the same way in all languages that support regular expressions.

If you are unfamiliar with it, an example (or a few) might help understand the concept.

■ **Note** Regular expression is sometimes shortened to regex or regexp.

7.1 Searching Within a File

Problem

Suppose you have a data file with some names, such as

```
Albert Sodir
Rohan Garner
Rana Roy
Alan Donald
Bobby Rosales
Sunil Pande
Raja Sen
Alisha Fitzerald
Amir Hussain
Anand Patnaik
```

© Malay Mandal 2016
M. Mandal, *Ruby Recipes*, DOI 10.1007/978-1-4842-2469-4_7

First name and last name are separated by a single space. If you want to find the names (first names) that start with the letter A, it would be easy.

The following program identifies and prints the names that start with an A.

```
infile = File.open 'names.txt','r'
while line = infile.gets
        if line[0] == 'A'
                puts line
        end
end
infile.close
```

The if part could have been written more succinctly without any loss of functionality.

```
puts line if line.start_with?('A')
```

start_with? is a String function that tests if the string starts with the given substring, and then returns a Boolean.

To find the names that start with either 'A' or 'B', you need a slight extension on the if condition (the earlier form of the if).

```
if line[0] == 'A' or line[0] == 'B'
```

You get the right result.

```
Albert Sodir
Alan Donald
Bobby Rosales
Alisha Fitzerald
Amir Hussain
Anand Patnaik
```

If someone were to ask you to work with 'C' also, the condition would extend further. At the point where it would become any character from 'A' to 'Z', you could have 26 such conditions joined with or, (or you could drop the if condition altogether, hoping that all names will start with a capital letter anyway, and it can only be any letter from A to Z).

If you were to have a set A to Y, you could just check a single condition under such circumstances: that the name does not start with Z.

```
if line[0] != 'Z'
```

If you were to exclude two characters (such as Y and Z), you would have to join the individual (not) conditions with and. Such is the nature of logical operations.

```
if line[0] != 'Y' and line[0] != 'Z'
```

152

Things get trickier if you want to find names that start with any letter from N to Z. And I have not put in the condition yet, which specifies that they could be either lowercase or uppercase.

In this case, you can do it with 13 individual equality comparisons, joined by 'or'. That would not be a pretty site, and probably not as much fun to type either (and that's just for uppercase letters).

Is there any easier way to do this?

Solution

You could use the following code.

```
infile = File.open 'names.txt','r'
while line = infile.gets
        puts line if line.match(/^[N-Z]/)
end
infile.close
which produces
Rohan Garner
Rana Roy
Sunil Pande
Raja Sen
```

line.match(/^[N-Z]/) substitutes 13 comparisons joined with or.

How It Works

The part between / and / (which is ^[N-Z]) indicates a pattern (in this case, the pattern is expressed with a regular expression). In a sense, / and / can be thought of as defining pattern boundary.

LANGUAGE WITHIN LANGUAGE

Before the explanation of this particular expression, let's get into a bit of terminology. A regular expression is usually used to search something (a pattern) within something (typically a string).

In our case, even though the whole file is searched, only one line at a time is picked up in the pattern search. So the source string is the current line (or a single line, if you would like to think about it that way).

But what is our pattern?

Patterns described as regular expressions have their own language of expression— as if it is a language within language. Fortunately, most standard programming or scripting languages that support regular expressions follow uniform symbolism to express such expressions (i.e., to describe such patterns). So if you master one language, you should be able to utilize the knowledge more readily when it comes to implementing another language.

The expression ^[N-Z] in our pattern can be seen as having two parts. The first part (consisting of ^) is an anchor (or positional indicator) that represents where (in the source string) to look for the given pattern (**anchor => "where to look for"**). The second part (consisting of [N-Z]) indicates a range of possible characters applied to a single character (i.e., that single character could be one of any characters in the range of characters specified). This part specifies "what to look for."

The particular anchor (^) means that at the beginning of the source string (or immediately after the beginning, if you prefer to think of it that way) and the particular N-Z range specifies any capital letter from N to Z (inclusive of both). The [ ] construct (which by itself means a single occurrence) specifies to look for a single character (in the source string).

If we were to build a translation table for the regular expression ^[N-Z] (as if we are translating the language of regular expression to English to understand what it is saying), it would look like Table 7-1.

Table 7-1. *Regular Expressions Translated to English*

Expression	English Equivalent
[ ]	Any single character
N-Z	Which is anything in between (capital) N and (capital) Z (both inclusive)
^	And occurs at the beginning (of the source string)

You can easily extrapolate that an a-d range specifies any letter among a, b, c, or d (lowercase).

Putting it together, the regular expression ^[N-Z] means this: look for any single capital letter in the range N to Z (both inclusive) at the beginning of the source string.

A six-character regular expression means a lot in English. Imagine a politician who talks a lot. What would happen if he were compelled to talk in regular expressions. How much would he say in an hour? (If that happens, surf away from the news channels.)

Regular expression has many aspects, two of which you have been introduced to already (***anchor*** and ***range***). Note that ^ is not the only anchor; there are others.

Anchors and ranges are not the only facets of regular expressions, however. There is a lot more to it.

7.2 Finding Only the Matched String

Problem

In our earlier code we were simply printing the entire line if it had a match.

```
puts line if line.match(/^[N-Z]/)
```

What if we were interested in getting only the part that matched (namely, the first character when it falls within the range N to Z), not the entire line?

Solution

The following code works fine.

```
infile = File.open 'names.txt','r'
while line = infile.gets
        if matched = line.match(/(^[N-Z])/)
                retarr = matched.captures
                puts retarr[0]
        end
end
infile.close
```

It produces this:

```
R
R
S
R
```

These are the first letters from the names Rohan, Rana, Sunil, and Raja.

How It Works

Take a look at the following code.

```
if matched = line.match(/(^[N-Z])/)
        retarr = matched.captures
        puts retarr[0]
end
```

Note that the **pattern itself has parentheses** (^[N-Z]) is enclosed within a set of parentheses. This set of parentheses indicates a group boundary.

A *group* is defined as follows: A whole pattern may have one (or more) part(s) captured as a group (i.e., within parentheses) and optionally other parts, out of

groups (i.e., we could have said something like /(^[N-Z])A/, which means one single letter between N and Z in the beginning, followed by A). A string that has 'RA' at the beginning will match that pattern; however, since the ^[N-Z] is in parentheses, which matches the 'R' part of 'RA', only the 'R' character (not 'A') will be captured as a group.

The function match returns a MatchData object, which contains matched data (or nil if no match is found). Don't be concerned about the MatchData class for now.

If nil is returned (i.e., no match is found for a line), the condition of if evaluates to nil (or false), and the if block is skipped.

If it has a match, the matched part is caught in the matched object. The retarr array gets all the substrings from the source string, which is matched by the groups within the pattern (in this case, only one group and only one substring per matched line). The first element from the array—that is, the first substring—as captured upon group matching, (in this case the only sub-string per matched line)is printed to the console.

As an aside, the code could have been further simplified.

```
puts retarr[0]
```

could have been replaced with

```
puts retarr
```

Since the first element is the only element in the array, the output would be identical. However, retarr[0] possibly emphasizes the fact that captures returns an array of strings, not a single string.

Instead of taking the captured groups (in this case, group) in an array, it could have been printed directly. The following two lines could have been combined into one.

```
retarr = matched.captures
puts retarr[0]
```

As shown here.

```
puts  matched.captures
```

If matched is evaluated before the if, and the if block becomes a single statement, the if and condition could come after the statement (and the end taken out). The program could then be written like this:

```
infile = File.open 'names.txt','r'
while line = infile.gets
        matched = line.match(/(^[N-Z])/)
        puts matched.captures if matched
end
infile.close
```

You may prefer this form over the other. It is a matter of personal choice.

7.3 Working with Character Classes

Problem

You have an input file (named desc.txt) containing the following two lines.

```
A Tale
of Two Cities
```

How do you get the characters (from each of those lines) that match either A, B, or C (each in uppercase)?

Solution

Run the following code on the file.

```
infile = File.open 'desc.txt','r'
while line = infile.gets
        matched = line.match(/([ABC])/)
        puts matched.captures
end
infile.close
```

It produces the following.

```
A
C
```

How It Works

In the context of regular expressions, a character class is a set of characters enclosed within square brackets. It specifies the characters that will successfully match a single character from a given input string. A character class matches any one of a set of characters.

■ **Note**   A single pattern (without any quantifier or other instruction to repeat the pattern search) always stops after the very first match (assuming that a match is found; otherwise, it will scan the whole source string and return nil where applicable).

Here [ABC] is a character class that specifies the following: match a character (the very first character of that kind; in the line, in this case) that is either A or B or C. (And note that regular expressions are very much case sensitive).

In the first line, the first such character is the very first character. It finds A and is done with the search.

In the second line, the very first letter is 'o' and it is not capitalized. The first capital letter is 'T', which does not qualify because it is not either A or B or C. The first letter that qualifies is the 'C' of Cities.

Let's say that we were to make it anchored (i.e., we were to change the pattern as follows).

```
matched = line.match(/(^[ABC])/)
```

The addition of the ^ anchor prior to the character class means that the search is to be restricted to the first character only. Run the program (after saving the file, of course). You get an error like this:

```
abcmatch.rb:4:in `<main>': undefined method `captures' for nil:NilClass
(NoMethodError)
```

This is because no match is found in the second line. (The first character is not A or B or C in the second line). Hence, it returns nil. **Calling** captures **on a** nil **object causes the error.**

To fix the error, you can add an if condition to the puts line (which makes the code call the captures method only when a proper match is found, but not on nil).

```
infile = File.open 'desc.txt','r'
while line = infile.gets
        matched = line.match(/(^[ABC])/)
        puts matched.captures if matched
end
infile.close
```

In this case, however, no output is printed for the second line of input.

A

Negation

The previous example was a simple character class. But there are other types.

If you needed to specify, for instance, that the pattern would not be one of a few alternatives (not either A or B or C), you could use the [^ABC] pattern instead of [ABC]. The code line containing pattern would then be as follows.

```
matched = line.match(/([^ABC])/)
```

And upon execution, a space would be matched for the first line and the letter 'o' would be identified in the second line. The space is the first non-ABC (not A or B or C) character in the first line.

Note that the ^ symbol has a completely different meaning here (inside [ ]). It does not represent an anchor but negation.

Range

You have already encountered range. If you wish something to match any capital letter between N and Z (both inclusive), the pattern should be defined as [N-Z].

■ **Note** This covers range as applicable to regular expressions. It has nothing to do with the Range data type in Ruby. Remember "language within language."

Suppose that for the desc.txt data file discussed earlier, you are to get any characters either from A to E or from R to Z. How do you do this? (For now, suspend the judgement as to why we should look for such a weird range of characters.)

Ranges can be concatenated. For instance, if you want a character class to match anything from A to E and then R to Z, you could write that as [A-ER-Z] (as simple as that).

Upon running on the input file, the following code

```
infile = File.open 'desc.txt','r'
while line = infile.gets
        matched = line.match(/([A-ER-Z])/)
        puts matched.captures if matched
end
infile.close
```

produces this:

```
A
T
```

For the first line, the very first character was good enough ('A' is between A and E inclusive). In the second line, the first one that matched is 'T' of the word 'Two' (which is between R and Z inclusive).

For any capital or lowercase letter, the range should be defined as [A-Za-z] (or [a-zA-Z], which is equivalent).

You may try a range like [Z-A] to see what happens.

Union

If you are to look for an union of two sets of characters (say, two ranges) you could nest the square brackets containing one set within another, like [A-Z[a-z]].

Note that if both are ranges, it is equivalent to contiguous ranges, as shown earlier. That is, [A-Z[a-z]] is equivalent to [A-Za-z]. There are other cases where they would be equivalent.

Intersection

From the input file (desc.txt), how do you find any character that is the intersection of the set of letters A to V (set1) and T to Z (set 2)?

You could find out the intersecting set and use it as a range. But suppose you don't want to think so much? You'd rather let the program do it.

The intersection of two sets of characters could be defined with the construct.

```
[<set1>&&[<set2>]]
```

This is an example.

```
[A-V&&[T-Z]]
```

The [A-V&&[T-Z]] pattern matches any single character, which is common to the range A–V and T–Z (which is T–V).

It's no wonder that the following code identifies 'T' from both lines. (This is the only available capital letter in either line in the range T–V).

```
infile = File.open 'desc.txt','r'
while line = infile.gets
        matched = line.match(/([A-V&&[T-Z]])/)
        puts matched.captures if matched
end
infile.close
```

Intersection with Negation

It gets interesting when you mix intersection with negation. It could be helpful when you have a big range, but only a few characters are to be left out (all except).

Suppose that you wanted to extract all lowercase letters, except vowels, from the same input file. How do you do it?

The [a-z&&[^aeiou]] pattern works well.

The following code

```
infile = File.open 'desc.txt','r'
while line = infile.gets
        matched = line.match(/([a-z&&[^aeiou]])/)
        puts matched.captures if matched
end
infile.close
```

produces 'l' and 'f', respectively, from the two lines. You may verify that those are the first (or only) lowercase consonants.

This would eventually work with two ranges, such as [A-V&&[^T-Z]].

An intersection with negation, where the inner set is a complete subset of the outer set, may be termed as *subtraction*. In our earlier example of matching lowercase constants, the pattern used was a subtraction pattern; however, the same cannot be said for [a-j&&[^aeiou]].

Common Character Classes

Table 7-2 offers a quick reference for some common character classes.

Table 7-2. *A Quick Reference for Some Common Character Classes*

Construct	Meaning
[ABC]	A, B, or C (simple class)
[^ABC]	Any character except A,B, or C (negation)
[A-Z]	Any character from A to Z, both ends inclusive (range)
[A-Za-z]	Any character from A to Z or any character from a to z (contiguous ranges)
[A-P[N-S]]	Union of characters from A to P and N to S (union)
[A-Z&&[DEF]]	Intersection of characters from A to Z (inclusive) and the characters D,E, and F; effectively only D, E, and F (intersection)
[A-Z&&[^D-F]]	Any characters from A to Z (both ends inclusive) except any characters from D to F (inclusive of both ends) (subtraction)

Predefined Character Classes

Table 7-3 provides a quick reference of some predefined character classes. They are shorthand for some commonly used regular expressions.

Table 7-3. *A Quick Reference of Some Predefined Character Classes*

Construct	Meaning
.	Any character (but not usually the line terminator)
\d	A digit [0-9]
\D	A non-digit [^0-9]
\s	A whitespace character: [\t\n\x0B\f\r] (includes spaces, tabs, and newline, among other things).
\S	A non-whitespace character
\w	A word character [A-Za-z0-9_]
\W	A non-word character

The meaning of the words *digits*, *non-digits* (characters other than digits), and *character* (by negation, not a word character) should be pretty intuitive. Some words are less intuitive. Let's start with . (dot).

Any Single Character: dot

The . (dot) is a predefined character class. It represents a wildcard that matches any single character (except a line terminator, unless indicated by a modifier; discussed later in the book).

To see how it works, run the following code.

```
infile = File.open 'desc.txt','r'
while line = infile.gets
        matched = line.match(/(.)/)
        puts matched.captures
end
infile.close
Which will come up with
A
o
```

No wonder it identified the first characters from each line.

Note that for dot, you should not use the square braces. If you do, an error is encountered upon running the code.

Ranges (single or contiguous) should be enclosed within square braces.

Whitespace and Non-Whitespace

To illustrate that \s matches a whitespace character (in this case the first space in each line), you may run the following code.

```
infile = File.open 'desc.txt','r'
while line = infile.gets
        matched = line.match(/(\s)/)
        puts "-" + matched.captures[0] + "-"
end
infile.close
```

This comes up with the following.

```
- -
- -
```

The '-' characters at either end make the space pronounced. The reason that matched.captures[0] has to be concatenated is because captures returns an array, which cannot be directly concatenated to strings. The first element (index 0) of that array, however, is a string, so that can be concatenated in the way shown. Try removing the [0] and the program will not run successfully.

In the first line of the input file, replace the first space with a tab and run the program.

```
A       Tale
```

The output is somewhat different (for obvious reason).

```
-        -
- -
```

Try putting a space (first) and then a tab between A and Tale. The output is the same as before. The space is picked up in this case.

Now restore the input file to its original condition and replace the \s in the code with \S (for non-whitespace characters). Upon running the code, the first letters are picked up on pattern match.

```
-A-
-o-
```

This won't change if you use a number of contiguous spaces and tabs at the beginning of these input lines. It will still match the first non-whitespace character in each line.

Special Characters

There are special characters that have significance in text parsing and processing. They start with a backslash. Notable among them are the following.

- \n – newline

- \r – carriage return

- \t - tab

- \b – backspace

- \f – form feed

- \a – bell\alert

You will likely deal most often with \t and \n, or \r\n taken together. In fact, for many line by line operations in text parsing, you will not need to bother with \n (or \r\n) because it is effectively the record separator. If, however, you bring a text file created in Windows to, say, Unix, you may have to get rid of the \r characters.

Some of these characters have interesting histories. Exploring a bit of that can help you understand why the record separator may be '\r\n' instead of just '\n'.

Back in the old days of ASR-33 teletypes or dot-matrix printers with traveling printheads, the CR (carriage return) literally returned the carriage to the left on a typewriter, and the NL(new line) advanced the paper. The machinery could overlap the operation if the CR came before an LF, so CR-LF, (i.e. \r\n) was the (de facto) newline. If the operation was supposed to print back to front, it took much longer.

Unix was the first system to adopt \n as the standard line separator. DOS/Windows did not adopt it. That is why, unto this day, Windows text files may use '\r\n' as the de facto newline.

Escape Sequence

Let's look at handling characters with special meaning to express their literal representation.

There are tokens that represent a lot of things, such as a dot (.) to represent a single character, or and ^ to represent the beginning of a string.

What if you wanted to look for those characters at their literal face value? For example, you want to find an actual dot (.).

The approach is to use an escape sequence, which is a backslash (\), to escape the meaning of the character (and use it at face value). Thus, if you want to look for a dot, you would use /\./.

The following code

```
print "matched" if "a.b".match(/\./)
```

prints this:

```
matched
```

The following code, however, does not.

```
print "matched" if "ab".match(/\./)
```

This is true for all such control characters (+ ? . * ^ $ ( ) [ ] { } | \), which includes backslash itself. In order to look for a single backslash, you need to use two in the pattern. (i.e., \\).

7.4 Finding Significant Positions in a String

Problem

How do you find the very last characters of each line? How do you find the boundaries of words in a string?

Solution

You have seen the anchor for the beginning of the source string. You have also seen the . (dot) character class in action. What if you wanted to get the last character of each line? Anchors address issues of position in a string, with respect to some identifiable landmark (if I am allowed to use the word *landmark* in the context of a string), such as beginning of a source string, the end of a source string, word boundaries, and so forth. Think of anchoring of a ship, which is in some sense, tying it up at a certain location. Table 7-4 offers useful anchors.

Table 7-4. Some Useful Anchors

Expression/Indicator	Meaning
^	Start of string or line
$	End of string or line
\A	Start of string only
\Z	End of string but for the final terminator, if any
\z	End of string only
\B	Non word boundary
\b	Word boundary

■ **Note** In Table 7-4, the *string* refers to a source string (referred to as a *source string* in this book).

End of a Source String

You should use the . (dot), but you also need an anchor to indicate the end of the source string—and that is $ (the dollar sign).

Try the following program.

```
infile = File.open 'desc.txt','r'
while line = infile.gets
        matched = line.match(/(.$)/)
        puts matched.captures
end
infile.close
```

You won't be disappointed. ('e' and 's' are identified as the last characters for those two lines). Note, however, that the dollar sign appears after the dot (not before, as with the case of the other anchor). This is important. Regexp tokens maintain their relative position (wherever applicable) in the search, as they appear in the pattern.

- ^. says to look for the single character just after the beginning.

- .$ says to look for the single character just before the end (newline is effectively the record separator, so it isn't counted as part of the source string for this purpose).

That is how the first character and last character are specified in regexp.

165

Word Boundary and Non-Word Boundary

In order to understand the concept of word boundary, here is a bit of an explanation.

A word boundary (\b) is a zero-width match that can match:

- Between a word character (\w) and a non-word character (\W) or

- Between a word character and the start or end of the string.

Note that, by definition, a word character (\w) is [A-Za-z0-9_] (in general).

Take the string "bread and jam". The word boundary matches the (zero-width) places shown by the character '|'.

|bread|, |and| |jam|.

On the other hand, a non-word boundary character is anything (any character) except a word boundary (a negation of word boundaries).

It can match a zero-width place that is

- Between two word characters.

- Between two non-word characters.

- Between a non-word character and the start or end of the string.

- The empty string.

In the string "bread and jam", it matches the places shown with | in the following (any place that is not a word boundary, so the negation of the places shown earlier):

b|r|e|a|d,| a|n|d j|a|m.|

Note that in this example (non-word boundaries), if the full stop was not there after the word *jam*, then the end of the string would be a word boundary instead of a non-word boundary.

Now, let's look at some actual demonstration on our input file (consisting of).

```
A Tale
of Two Cities
```

Run the following code.

```
infile = File.open 'desc.txt','r'
while line = infile.gets
        matched = line.match(/(.\b)/)
        puts matched.captures
end
infile.close
```

It produces this:

```
A
f
```

'A' is the end of first word in the first line (the whole word consists of a single letter, and hence, that is also the last character). 'f' is the end of first word (in the second line), which is 'of'.

. \b says to get the single character just before the (applicable) word boundary; *applicable*, in this case, means the ***first such word boundary that has a character before it,*** not just the first word boundary, because it is looking for a pattern that is a character followed by a word boundary (so, the first occurrence of such a combination).

If you were to change the pattern to \b. (i.e., a character followed by a word boundary) 'o' would be picked up instead of the 'f' in the second input line.

The following code (for a character followed by a non-word boundary)

```
infile = File.open 'desc.txt','r'
while line = infile.gets
        matched = line.match(/(.\B)/)
        puts matched.captures
end
infile.close
```

produces this:

```
T
o
```

For the first line, the first non-word boundary, preceded by a character, is the zero-width place after T (of the word Tale). In fact, that is the first non-word boundary in that line.

Start and End of a String

Let's explore how \A and \Z behave at the start and end of source string.
Try the following code.

```
infile = File.open 'desc.txt','r'
while line = infile.gets
        matched = line.match(/(.\A)/)
        puts matched.captures if matched
end
infile.close
```

Nothing significant happens because we are looking for a pattern at the beginning of the source string with a character before that. By definition, there should be no character before the beginning of the string (because if there was, the beginning would not be the beginning).

167

Change the pattern to \A.

```
matched = line.match(/(\A.)/)
```

You will get the very first characters from each line.

For the end of string pattern, there is no point in looking for a character after that. So look for a character prior to that instead.

■ **Note**   In the input file, there should be only two lines (not an empty third line). The second line should not be terminated with a new line in the input file at this point.

The following code

```
infile = File.open 'desc.txt','r'
while line = infile.gets
        matched = line.match(/(.\Z)/)
        puts matched.captures if matched
end
infile.close
```

comes up with this:

```
e
s
```

If there is a newline at the end of a line, \z possibly matches that and does not return anything. My recommendation is try using \Z or $ as the case may be, and avoid \z (as far as possible).

Interaction of Subpatterns

Let's look at how parts of a pattern work in combination to make up the whole pattern.

In order to get the first character, you can use the ^. pattern.

In order to get the first two characters, you should use the ^.. pattern.

To illustrate this, run the following code.

```
print "test string".match(/(^.)/).captures
puts
print "test string".match(/(^..)/).captures
```

It produces this:

```
["t"]
["te"]
```

Note that for this code, no input data file is needed. It runs on the string specified (in the code itself). A couple of print statements have been used. This does not add a newline by itself at the end (and it prints the output as an array where applicable).

The puts in the second line separates the output of the two print statements in two different lines (to add a newline).

The output illustrates my point. The first two characters have been identified.

■ **Note** Regarding the 'one way': there are other ways to achieve the same result using regexp.

It does not take much imagination to understand what is needed for the first three characters. However, if we wanted the first two characters *after* the 't' character, the following code will work.

```
print "test string".match(/t(..)/).captures
```

It produces the following output.

```
["es"]
```

Note that if you were to put the 't' within the group,

```
print "test string".match(/(t..)/).captures
```

you get the following instead.

```
["tes"]
```

But our goal is to get the characters following and excluding the **applicable** 't'. Hence, it should be outside the group, although it should be part of the search pattern.

The word *applicable* is significant here. Regular expression has its own language in a way. And you need to express your thoughts (about the pattern you are looking for) in that language. So it is important to understand what you are asking it to do (or rather to make sure that what you are asking it to do is indeed what you want done).

To illustrate it more clearly, if you think that /t(..)/ describes a pattern that matches the first 't' that it gets, and then two characters after that, you are wrong. It matches the **first occurrence of any such 't' that has two characters following it**.

This means that if the string has a 't' in it but no such 't' has (at least) two characters following it, the match will not be successful. For instance, the following code

```
print "tt".match(/(t..)/).captures
```

results in an error.

```
... undefined method `captures' for nil:NilClass ...
```

It is important to understand that multiple subpatterns within a regular expression are added up to make the pattern (that is, the thing being looked for) lengthier. When you are looking for just a 't' or just an 'e', it can just look for that. However, when you are asking to look for 't' followed by 'e', it has to look for 'te', and no matter how many separate t's and e's are in the source string, if no combination is found where an 'e' follows a 't', then your search is unsuccessful.

It is neither good nor bad. You just need to specify what you are looking for in the right manner.

Looking for Multiple Groups

The captures function returns an array of a string that matched all the groups in the pattern (in that order). If only one group is specified and the match is successful, only that group is returned. In order to capture multiple groups, you can ask for multiple groups in the pattern.

The following code

```
print "iteration".match(/t(...)t(...)/).captures
```

prints this:

```
["era", "ion"]
```

The pattern can be translated as follows.

1. Find the first such 't' that has three characters following it.

2. Capture those three characters in the first group.

3. Find the next 't', which should be immediately following (immediately following the three characters that follow the first such t) and which itself should be followed by three characters (at least).

4. Capture those three characters (in the second group).

■ **Note**   Characters do not include newline.

Here the pattern was chosen in such a manner that there was a second t following a first t, and three characters after that. If that t was not there, the match would fail. In order for this pattern to work, there has to be at least eight characters, the first and fifth of which should be 't'.

The last code was meant to show how multiple groups can be captured. **It should be noted, however, that the groups presented within the pattern combine with other parts of the pattern (in the given order) to form a complete pattern, and unless the whole pattern is present, the match will fail.**

7.5 Using Non-Capturing Groups

Problem

You may wish that a second group be part of the pattern (to indicate the alternatives) but not be captured. How can you do that?

What would happen if we used captures on ["white and black".match (/(wh(eat|ite))/)]? What's the point in trying to guess, when it can easily be found out (by using captures and seeing what happens, for instance)?

The following code

```
print "white and black".match(/(wh(eat|ite))/).captures
```

prints this:

```
["white", "ite"]
```

It has captured two group matches. The second group is the one nested (i.e., (eat|ite), of which 'ite' is a match).

Solution

This can be accomplished by making the group passive (or non-capturing). The way to do that is to put a '?:' at the beginning of the group.

The following code

```
print "white and black".match(/(wh(?:eat|ite))/).captures
```

prints this:

```
["white"]
```

This will work even when the groups are not nested. For example, the following

```
print "white,black, or yellowish".match(/(white)(.*)(yellow).*/).captures
```

prints this:

```
["white", ",black, or ", "yellow"]
```

Yet, the following code

```
print "white,black, or yellowish".match(/(white)(?:.*)(yellow).*/).captures
```

prints this:

```
["white", "yellow"]
```

171

7.6 Understanding the Regex Engine and Backtracking

Problem

Having some idea about how a regex engine works would help you understand the functioning of certain pattern constructs more clearly.

The phrase "regex engine" is in wide circulation. On the Internet, you can find plenty of pages refereeing to it. Getting familiar with the term is likely to help your further studies on the subject of regular expressions.

Solution

What is a regular expression engine? I did not find a very clear definition on the Internet. I am providing an overview from my own understanding (which is by no means an official definition, but in this regard, understanding is far more important, in my view, than an official definition).

The engine in this sense refers to **part of the Ruby language's operating environment (which may consist of a compiler/interpreter and an execution platform). In this book, it is referred to as ROE (Ruby Operating Environment), which deals with interpreting regular expressions as they appear in a pattern (check validity), trying to find one or more match(es) as requested, and capturing the group.** It may be helpful to think of this part of ROE as a separate executive performing due diligence on source strings and patterns, and handing out reports. (Although it really isn't separate, this is a matter of convenience for discussion and understanding.)

And how does the engine work? There is more than one type of regular expression engine. However, because this is not a reference book, let's not get into too much detail. Besides, for day-to-day use, you probably won't need a very deep level of understanding the engine. So I will try to keep it simple and try to provide an overview based on my understanding.

The following are two basic rules that apply in general, for the engine:

- The first match wins

- Patterns are inherently greedy

The engine

1. Runs from left to right for both the source string and for the pattern to be matched

2. Tries to match the whole pattern at each possible position (as applicable) in the whole source string, before going to the next position.

If it finds a match, it stops without checking any further (unless otherwise specified in the pattern).

In context of 'position (as applicable)', note that it is contextual (as per the pattern expression). For instance, if the pattern specifies a beginning anchor (^), if the match is not found in the very first position, there is no point in going ahead.

The possible positions in the source strings (in general) are the zero-length positions prior to each character, including each space, and the position at the end. So, in a "Hello World" string, the positions (shown with '|' character) are |H|e|l|l|o| |W|o|r|l|d|.

Plane Forward Search

This following explanation is based on a pattern that is a set of plane characters, but the principle applies to other patterns too (as applicable).

When the engine picks up the source string, on one hand (in a metaphorical sense), and the pattern, on the other, it starts with the first possible place (the zero-length position before the first character) in the source string. It tries to match that with the first character of the pattern. If a match is found, it goes ahead one position in the source string and tries to match that with the second character of the pattern. If that succeeds, it goes ahead one position further in source string and tries with the third character in the pattern, and so on.

If at one stage a match fails, it abandons the *basic starting position* in the source string (in this case, the first position) and moves ahead to the next position in the source string and tries to match the whole pattern starting from there. **(The "basic starting position" is not a commonly recognized term in this regard. I used it in this book for ease of description (and possible understanding.)**

If it succeeds in matching the whole pattern in a position, it returns success (or whatever the equivalent, as per implementation) and stops.

An example of a search on the string "Raca the cat, jumped in the hat" for the pattern /cat/ will help.

The search starts at the position before R, and tries to first match 'R' with the very first character in the pattern (which is 'c'), and fails. It advances to the next position, which is after 'R' and before 'a'. In its journey, at one point it comes to before (the first) 'c' in the source string.

This time, it tries to match 'c' (of 'Raca') with 'c' (from the pattern) and finds a match. It advances position and tries to match 'a' with 'a' (from the pattern) and succeeds. However, the next match between a space (from the source string) and 't' (from the pattern) fails. It gives up the current **basic starting position**, which is the place before 'c' in the word 'Raca' and makes the position after the 'c' its basic starting position for the next search attempt.

This goes on until it comes to just before the 'c' of the word 'cat' in the source string (assuming that the computer does not crash). At this point, it matches 'c' with 'c', goes ahead and matches 'a' with 'a', still goes ahead and matches 't' with 't'. And it concludes its journey.

Backtracking

Things may get more interesting when the pattern is more complex. Take the example of a pattern involving alternatives, such as /tra(in|ck)/ (which should match either 'train' or 'track') on the string "The trap set for Coltrain in the track".

At a point, when the engine has more than one option to find a suitable match for the next character (or subpattern, etc.), it remembers the other options that it can try. It also notes the position where the fork happened to get back and try the next alternative from that fork in the road, should the current alternative come to a dead end prior to completing a match. This is known as *backtracking* (coming back to the fork in the road and trying a previously untried alternative).

So, as it happens, the engine (or shall we say the car) sometimes runs in reverse (metaphorically speaking) as necessary.

Coming back to our example, although the search starts from the position prior to 'T', the real position of interest (for the current explanation) is the position prior to the 't' of 'trap'. The 't' the 'r' and the 'a', matches one by one from the pattern. Just before 'p' the engine has two options. Let's say it picks 'in' to try first and saves 'ck' for future search should 'in' fail. (This does not necessarily happen left to right, and follows a LIFO structure for getting the next alternative to try). Eventually 'p' does not match 'i' and the match fails. It *backtracks* to the position before 'p' and tries to match that with 'c' of 'ck'. Still fails. Now since it has no other untried alternative, it abandons the basic starting position (which is the position before the 't' of 'trap' in this case) and advances to the position after that 't' (i.e. before the 'r' of 'trap') and makes that it's basic starting position for the next attempt.

When it comes to the position before the 't' of 'Coltrain', things get interesting again. The 'tra' part matches as usual, it notes the position (as a fork in the road [metaphorically speaking]), saves the other alternative (say, 'ck'), and tries to find a further match for the 'in' part—character by character. And it finds a match. No need to backtrack any more. The pattern matches the 'train' part from the word 'Coltrain'.

More on Greedy (Meta-) Characters

In a fairy tale world, where metacharacters such as '*' and '+' (of regular expressions) are characters (in the story), you would find that they are greedy with acquiring and do not give up easily. The only time they backtrack and give up is when they have to do so for the team (read the subsequent part of the current search advances), and even that is as little as they can give away before getting away with it.

Consider the following code.

```
print "tatta".match(/.*a/)
```

It prints this:

```
tatta
```

And the following code

```
print "tatta".match(/.*at/)
```

prints this:

```
tat
```

In the first case, the `.*` initially takes up the whole string. Since the engine needs to match the 'a' from the pattern (following `.*`), the engine backtracks by one character from what is already matched (which prior to the backtrack, was the entire source string), and from that position it tries to *match next character in the source string* (which is 'a') *with the next character of the pattern* which is 'a'. The match succeeds, and hence, the whole string matches the entire pattern.

In the second case, however, the matching for `.*` takes the entire string, and then backtracking one character and matching the next 'a' character also succeeds. But at this point, the 't' (of the pattern) cannot be matched. So it has to backtrack more. In the process of backtracking, it reaches the (zero-length) position, after the first 't' in the source string, and tries to match forward the next characters of the source string ('a') and that of the pattern ('a'), it succeeds. From that position, it tries to match forward the next characters from the source string, and the next character from the pattern, both of which are 't', and the match succeeds. Hence, the entire pattern matches with 'tat'.

I hope that this provides a somewhat workable overview of how the engine operates.

7.7 Finding Repeated Patterns

Problem

You want to match patterns such as `'ab0ab0ab'` or `'cd1cd1cd'` or `'ef1ef1ef'` and so on, but not `'ab1cd1cd'` or `'cd2ab2ef'` and so on. How do you specify that?

Solution

A *backreference* is a type of construct in regular expressions. It provides a convenient way to identify a repeated character or substring within the source string. As far as backreferences are concerned, the key word is *repetition.*

Suppose you are looking for a `/(ab/cd/ef)/` pattern that will match either `'ab'` or `'cd'` or `'ef'`. However, you want to see whether the same pattern is repeating twice more after another character gap each time.

You can use (numbered) backreferences for the purpose.

The following code

```
print "matched" if "ab1ab2ab".match(/(ab|cd|ef).\1.\1/)
```

prints this:

```
matched
```

And the following code

```
print "matched" if "cd1cd2cd".match(/(ab|cd|ef).\1.\1/)
```

prints this:

```
matched
```

But the following code does not.

```
print "matched" if "ab1cd2cd".match(/(ab|cd|ef).\1.\1/)
```

How It Works

In the last code, the initial pattern found is 'ab' (even though it was looking for either 'ab' or 'cd' or 'ef'), and hence, the value of backreference \1 is set to 'ab' only. In the next case, after a gap of one character (signified by .), 'ab' does not occur, and hence, the entire pattern fails to match.

If you removed the last backreference and the preceding dot from the pattern (i.e., it was defined as /(ab|cd|ef).\1/), it would pass, however.

The following code

```
print "matched" if "ab1cd2cd".match(/(ab|cd|ef).\1/)
```

prints this:

```
matched
```

The match is not between 'ab' and 'cd' but between the last two 'cd''s. This becomes apparent upon running the following code.

```
print "ab1cd2cd".match(/(ab|cd|ef).\1/)
```

That prints the following.

```
cd2cd
```

You can have multiple backreferences in a single pattern, referring to *captured* groups, specified in that order in the pattern. Hence, the following code

```
print "matched" if "ab1cd2ef3cdabef".match(/(ab).(cd).(ef).\2\1\3/)
```

prints this:

```
matched
```

The three groups captured (in that order) set the values 'ab' to \1, 'cd' to \2 and 'ef' to \3, respectively. Hence, \2\1\3 translates to 'cdabef'. The rest should be easily understandable.

Any small deviation in this part of the string (assuming that you are not adding the same string elsewhere in the source string) interferes with the match.

Note that backreferences happens only with captured groups. If you were to make the second group non capturing; for example,

```
print "matched" if "ab1cd2ef3cdabef".match(/(ab).(?:cd).(ef).\2\1\3/)
```

An error will occur.

```
... invalid backref number/name: /(ab).(?:cd).(ef).\2\1\3/
```

This is because, the second group now being non-capturing. \2 actually gets the value captured from the third group, and \3 is meaningless (there are only two backreferences generated in this case).

An observation from this is that you cannot refer to an invalid backreference (one that is not generated from the pattern).

Octal Codes and Backreferences

In this context, it is worth mentioning *octal codes*. In Ruby, an octal code is distinguished by a preceding backslash. Hence, the following code

```
print "\121"
```

prints this:

Q

The question is how the Ruby compiler/executor environment knows whether such a number is an octal code or a backreference.

The following rules apply.

- The expressions \1 through \9 are always interpreted as backreferences and not as octal codes.

- If the first digit of a multi-digit expression starts with 8 or 9, the expression is interpreted as a literal.

- Expressions from \10 onward (except the 8 and 9 beginning digits) are considered backreferences if there is a backreference corresponding to that number; otherwise, they are treated as octal codes.

So you cannot get away with an invalid backreference if it is between \1 and \9 (both digits included).

As per the second point, the following code

```
print "\89"
```

prints this:

89

Named Backreferences

A named backreference is captured with the (?<name>pattern) construct and refereed with the \k<name> construct.

Suppose that you want to deal with two backreferences, and instead of referring to them as \1 and \2, you want to use names 'Hansel' and 'Gretel', respectively.

The following will work.

```
print "matched" if "cd1abcab3cd".match(/(?<Hansel>cd).(?<Gretel>ab).
\k<Gretel>.\k<Hansel>/)
```

In the first group, the whole construct, which is of the form (?<name>pattern), is represented by name 'Hansel' and the 'cd' pattern. The matched substring is 'cd', which is assigned to the backreference named Hansel, and can later be invoked as \k<Hansel>.

The following is the equivalent of our earlier code (with numbered backreferences).

```
print "matched" if "cd1cd2cd".match(/(ab|cd|ef).\1.\1/)
```

It can be written in the named backreference parlance, as follows.

```
print "matched" if "cd1cd2cd".match(/(?<x>ab|cd|ef).\k<x>.\k<x>/)
```

The choice of the name 'x' is arbitrary here (the name 'y' could serve equally well, if it is used consistently).

7.8 Finding a Match and Excluding Some of It in the Result

Problem

If you wished to match *qu* you could use the pattern /qu/. So long as it is purely for determining whether there is a match, it can be done as follows.

```
print "matched" if "aqua".match(/qu/)
```

If you are to get the matched string in return, you could use this:

```
print "aqua".match(/qu/)
```

It prints the following.

```
qu
```

But what if you wanted to print a 'q' on match, only if it has a u following it, but you did not want to get the u along with the returned value?

Solution

Things will get very tricky. If you just use the /q/ pattern, it will match even if there is no 'u' following the 'q'. And if you use /qu/ as pattern, the return value will contain 'qu'.

Note that the non-capturing group will not help you here because you are interested in the whole pattern, not individual groups.

So the following code

```
print "aqua".match(/q(?:u)/).captures
```

prints the following empty array, because the only group within the pattern is a passive (non-capturing) group.

```
[]
```

And this code:

```
print "aqua".match(/q(?:u)/)
```

prints the following.

```
qu
```

This is because the code is about the whole pattern, not the groups within.

Hmmm. How do you avoid the u (following the 'q') from being returned, while still checking for it as part of the match ?

The following code succeeds.

```
print "aqua".match(/q(?=u)/)
```

It prints this:

```
q
```

And the construct that is used— (?=sub-pattern)– is a ***lookahead assertion***.

I could not find a formal definition of assertions. In my own understanding, they can be expressed generally as the subpattern, presence, or absence of which (as specified), immediately ahead or behind another character or subpattern (as specified), causes the match to succeed, but which does not feature in the match returned. So it is essentially a subpattern that features in the search but does not feature in the returned value (along with some other characteristics).

Let's focus on ***presence or absence*** and ***ahead or behind.*** If we combine these two sets of possibilities, we can come up with four types of assertions.

- Present and ahead—or a ***lookahead assertion*** (an example of which has already been discussed)

- Not present ahead—or a ***negative lookahead assertion***

- Present and behind—or a *lookbehind assertion*
- Not present behind—or a *negative lookbehind assertion*

Negative Lookahead Assertion

Negative lookahead assertion uses the (?!sub-pattern) construct and **asks to look for a match if the subpattern specified in the assertion is not present (immediately) after the subpattern specified in the preceding parts in the pattern**. For instance, /q(?!u)/ means match a q only if it is not followed immediately by a 'u'.

The following code fails to match.

```
print "aqua".match(/q(?!u)/)
```

And this code:

```
print "aqa".match(/q(?!u)/)
```

prints as follows.

```
q
```

Lookbehind Assertion

You may have already guessed that lookbehind assertions talk about subpatterns, the presence or absence of which is considered preceding other subpatterns within the pattern. Lookbehind assertions **ask to look for a match if the subpattern in the assertion occurs (immediately) preceding the other relevant subpatterns within the pattern**.

The construct is (?<=sub-pattern) and in this case, it has to precede the other part in question. For instance, the /(?<=u)q/ pattern asks to match a q, which is immediately preceded by a 'u'.

The following code

```
print "auqa".match(/(?<=u)q/)
```

prints this:

```
q
```

Whereas the following code fails to match.

```
print "aqa".match(/(?<=u)q/)
```

Negative Lookbehind Assertion

Negative lookbehind assertion **asks to look for a match if the subpattern in the assertion does not occur (immediately) preceding the other relevant subpatterns within the pattern.** The construct used is (?<!sub-pattern) and it precedes the other relevant subpattern.

The /(?!=u)q/ pattern looks for a q only if it is not (immediately) preceded by 'u'. Eventually, the following code fails to match.

```
print "auqa".match(/(?<!u)q/)
```

And this code:

```
print "aqa".match(/(?<!u)q/)
```

prints as follows.

```
q
```

7.9 Inserting Comments in a Regular Expression

Problem

How do you insert comments in a regular expression?

Solution

Comments can be included in a Ruby regular expression. There is more than one way to do it.

A comment in a single line pattern uses the (?#comment) construct. For instance, the /te(?#this is a comment)/ pattern is effectively the same as /te/ as far as matching is concerned.

Eventually, the following code

```
print "test this".match(/te(?#st)/)
```

prints this:

```
te
```

Another way uses free-spacing mode. In this mode, a pattern is followed by an 'x' modifier and can be spread over multiple lines. The comment (at any line) starts at '#' and goes to the end of the line.

The following code

```
print "ababcabcd".match(/ab #the characters a and b
        c # followed by c
        a # and then another a/x)
```

is equivalent to the following, as far as match is concerned.

```
print "ababcabcd".match(/abca/)
```

It prints this:

```
abca
```

For a long and complicated pattern, this form of coding and commenting may greatly improve maintainability.

7.10 Modifying Results

Problem

You want your regular expression to work in a slightly different way from the default behavior. For example, if you are looking for an AB (both capital letters) pattern, you could use /AB/ for, and for lowercase you could use /ab/. Even for two letters, either case pattern requires four different combinations (/AB/,/ab/,/Ab/, /aB/). Is there a way that you could specify in the pattern that it should ignore case in the search?

You also want to include newlines in the results.

Solution

A modifier can be used in such instance. There are some modifiers available with regular expressions. They allow modifications for the representation or interpretation of the pattern. You were introduced to one modifier, which is the free-spacing modifier or the ignore whitespace modifier, which is represented by an x after the pattern (not included within the pattern).

There is an ignore-case modifier, represented by an 'I' after the pattern.

The following code

```
print "ababcabcd".match(/AB/i)
```

prints this:

```
ab
```

But the following code does not match anything (for understandable reasons).

```
print "ababcabcd".match(/AB/)
```

How It Works

Ignoring case behavior can be used on a subpattern, in which case it can be specified with a construct such as /R(?i)uby/ or /R(?i:uby)/– both of which match the word *Ruby* with 'uby' in any case.

So the following code

```
print "ababcabcd".match(/a(?i)BC/)
```

and

```
print "ababcabcd".match(/a(?i:BC)/)
```

are equivalent. They both print the following.

```
abc
```

Although the second construct is more useful, if there are other subpatterns following the "ignore case" where case should not be ignored.

The following code

```
print "ababcabcD".match(/a(?i:bc)D/)
```

prints this:

```
abcD
```

But the following code does not return a match.

```
print "ababcabcd".match(/a(?i:bc)D/)
```

This may be desirable (because you may want to match only when the 'D' is in capital, not otherwise). If you use the first construct, however, you will find a match on the source string in both cases.

The multiline modifier (indicated by an 'm' after the pattern) in Ruby is not really a multiline modifier by general standards. This is equivalent to single-line or DOTALL mode in some other implementations (usually indicated by an s after the pattern in those implementations) and simply means *dot (.) will match newlines also*.

Hence, the following code fails to match.

```
print "ababcabcd\n".match(/cd./)
```

Whereas this code:

```
print "ababcabcd\n".match(/cd./m)
```

prints the following.

```
cd
```

It is recommended that modifiers, especially the m modifier (in Ruby), be avoided for performance reasons.

7.11 Using Non-Backtracking Groups

Problem

You want the engine to throw away all backtracking positions remembered by any tokens inside the group. This may be especially helpful where fast-fail is desired to avoid a lot of extra effort for an attempted match that won't happen anyway.

Solution

Atomic groups with a (?>sub-pattern) construct are non-backtracking groups.

How It Works

To understand how it works, first consider the /a(bc|b)c/ pattern that will match either 'abc' or 'abcc'.

Now, if you make the alternative group an atomic one, the pattern becomes /a(?>bc|b)c/ and it will not match 'abc' anymore. Why?

In the source string "abc" and this pattern, the 'a' is a match to 'a'. Subsequently, the match is found for the 'bc' portion of the alternative, with the 'bc' part of the string. When it tries to find a match for the last 'c' in the pattern, it has already exited the group within the pattern, and in doing so, this being an atomic group, has discarded all backtracking positions that were applicable within the group. (So at this point, alternative 'b' will not be attempted for a match from the second position—that context is gone.) Since before coming to the last 'c' in the pattern, the whole source string "abc" has been used to match the prior part of the pattern (prior to the last 'c'), nothing is left to be matched by 'c'. (And having come out of the non-backtracking group, no backtracking will happen to release another character in this case). Hence, the overall pattern match fails.

```
print "ababcabcd".match(/(a(?>bc|b)c)/)
```

fails to match this:

```
print "ababcabcd".match(/(a(bc|b)c)/)
```

And prints this:

```
abc
```

An atomic group fails fast. If one of the alternatives for such a group has matched a part of the source string (at which point it exits the group) and the subsequent subpattern (outside the group) does not match, it gives up without trying any other alternatives. In certain situations, this is very helpful with avoiding unnecessary work.

If you have a pattern such as /\b(armchair|armour|army)\b/ to be matched on a "armchairperson" source string, it obviously won't match because of the ending word boundary. However, this being a normal group, backtracking will happen once the last '\b' in the pattern fails to match the 'p' in the source string, as it tries to match the alternative 'armchair' with the source string. It will try the other options, but in vain.

If the group is made an atomic one /\b(?>armchair|armour|army)\b/ as soon as the 'armchair' part is matched, the group exits. It fails to match '\b' and gives up without backtracking. Some effort is saved. In case where a batch program has the potential for a lot of such savings, it could add up to significant performance boost.

Consider, however, the /\b(?>arm|armchair|armour)\b/ pattern on the source string "armchair". In a normal group, it would match the alternative 'armchair'. However, the following code fails to match anything.

```
print "armchair".match(/\b(?>arm|armchair|armour)\b/)
```

This is not the desired behavior.

After matching the leftmost alternative, 'arm', with that part in the source string, the group exits (**"without a trace" in a manner of speaking**) and the subsequent '\b' fails to match. And there goes the entire match.

7.12 Replacing Substrings Using Regular Expressions

Problem

You need to replace part(s) of a string as you search for a particular pattern.

Take a look at the following string:

"All the land belongs to John Doe. All the horses belong to John Doe. And the farmhouse belongs to John Doe"

How would you replace "John Doe" with "me"?

Solution

You could do it this way.

```
print "All the land belongs to John Doe. All the horses belong to John Doe.
And the farmhouse belongs to John Doe".gsub(/John Doe/,'me')
```

The preceding code prints as follows.

```
All the land belongs to me. All the horses belong to me. And the farmhouse
belongs to me
```

It uses the gsub function (for global substitution) with two parameters. The first one is a pattern. The second one indicates the substring that should be used to replace each of the matches.

If you used the sub function instead of gsub in the same fashion, only the first occurrence of 'John Doe' would be replaced.

You may try this on a file level. On an input file containing

```
All the land belongs to John Doe.
All the horses belong to John Doe.
And the farmhouse belongs to John Doe
```

this code

```
infile = File.open 'inp.txt','r'
outfile = File.open 'outfile.txt','w'
while line = infile.gets
        outfile.print line.gsub(/John Doe/,'me')
end
infile.close
outfile.close
```

would produce this

```
All the land belongs to me.
All the horses belong to me.
And the farmhouse belongs to me
```

in the output file.

It is possible to use gsub, along with block structure, to do further processing prior to replacement, after the pattern is found. (Note that the gsub function was introduced in Recipe 2.15 in the context of manipulating strings).

The following code finds each number group (separated by spaces in between), converts the group to an integer, and doubles them prior to replacing them with the result (of doubling).

```
print "12 10 16".gsub(/(\d+)/) { |m| m.to_i * 2 }
```

It prints as follows.

```
24 20 32
```

7.13 Using the scan Function with Regular Expressions

The scan function was introduced in Recipe 2.15 the in context of manipulating strings. scan can also work with regular expressions.

You have already seen that the following code

```
print "this is the theatre".scan("th")
```

produces this:

```
["th", "th", "th"]
```

Try the following code.

```
str = "this is the theatre"
rslt = str.scan("th")
puts rslt.inspect
```

The result is the same. The `inspect` function offers an alternate means to inspect the result of the scan. (The function `to_s` also behaves the same way in the place of inspect here.)

Try a regular expression in place of a string for the scan (as shown next).

```
str = "this is the theatre"
rslt = str.scan(/t|h/)
puts rslt.inspect
```

The result is very different.

```
["t", "h", "t", "h", "t", "h", "t"]
```

Since `match` with regular expressions (unless otherwise specified) finds the first match, using `scan` with regular expressions may provide an easy way to find all the matches of the pattern in the source string.

Exercises

The solutions are in the appendix.

Exercise 7.1

Suppose you are interested in finding the names of people in sentences (programmatically). The idea is in a sentence (i.e., "Abani Sen mentioned that he will be absent on Thursday."), a person's name is identified as two consecutive words that start with a capitalized (the capital at the beginning but not elsewhere).

Write such a program (use one sentence at a time as input) and apply it to the preceding example sentence and to the sentence, "The US president, Barrack Obama, proposed the bill." From each sentence, take only the first name (if there is more than one).

■ **Hint** Use groups.

Exercise 7.2

An application tracking train timing prints into a log file. There are lines like this:

```
Train 45DN arrived at Strathfield station 13:04:22
Train 36UP departed from Redfern station 12:56:30
```

There are other lines in the log that are not of this format and not of interest to us.

The task is to find those lines and get the train number, station name, and arrival or departure time (the tokens).

Suppose the log file contains the following lines -

```
Train 36UP departed from Redfern station 12:56:30
received web request 12:57:20
response OK
Train 45DN arrived at Strathfield station 13:04:22
DB connection failure 13:11:32
```

Extract the relevant tokens and print the result

■ **Hint**   Use groups.

CHAPTER 8

■ ■ ■

Putting It into Action

In this chapter, a few more tasks are discussed. Many (or perhaps all) of them involve regular expressions.

8.1 Removing Block CommentedCode

Problem

The first task is rather easy. Suppose you have a Java project with multiple files in multiple subfolders (packages). You developed it little by little, experimenting with this and that. In the process, you commented a lot of functions entirely. Sometimes you commented a large chunk of code within a function. You are done with your experimentation; however, there is too much commented code. Not that it would do anyone any harm beyond a bit of disk space, etc.), but you want the code to be neat. Why bother to keep 3,000 lines of code if you can get away with 1,000 lines?

There are some comments, however, that you want to keep. For now, consider that you want to remove only block comments (which start with /* and end with */ and may span multiple lines). You want to keep line style comments (which start with //) because they may contain important descriptions for the developer (or maintainer)—unless, of course, those line style comments appear within a block comment, in which case they should be removed anyway.

Solution

For the purpose of coding and testing, just take two subdirectories at the same level (a and b) and have ab.java in a and def.java in b files. (Even if the files were in different subdirectory levels, the trick as to how to tackle them has already been covered).

```
a/abc.java
b/def.java
```

© Malay Mandal 2016
M. Mandal, *Ruby Recipes*, DOI 10.1007/978-1-4842-2469-4_8

For testing purposes, you don't need to write real Java code in those files. Put the following in the abc.java file.

```
//Project
import something.something;
/*  This is a comment  */
some more statements
/* This too
        is a commenting
spanning three lines */
good bye
```

Put the following in the def.java file.

```
//Project
Nothing to import
/*  This is a comment  */
few statements
and /* this too is */ a comment
/* This too
        is a commenting
        //having another comment trapped within
        */
        few more statements
        //Alternatively : instead of good bye you may say
see you
```

The art of comment removal can be perfected in one file first. Extending it to multiple files will not be difficult. For this purpose, def.java is the most suitable. So copy it in the current folder.

Reading the whole file at once makes the task easier. See the following code.

```
text = File.read('def.java')
text1 = text.gsub(/\/\*.*?\*\//m,'')
print text1
```

It prints like this:

```
//Project
Nothing to import

few statements
and   a comment

        few more statements
        //Alternatively : instead of good bye you may say
see you
```

190

It works almost correctly—*almost* because it leaves an empty line for two of the block comments in the input file (def.java).

The /\/*.*?*\// pattern generally means this: /*, any number of characters (without being greedy), and */. Since the file is read in one shot and the m modifier is used for the gsub (which causes the dot to match even newline characters), the multiline span is equivalent to a single line for the block comments.

The non-greedy specification is needed because otherwise it will start at the first /* and end at the last */ (the end of last block comment), taking everything in between. You may test that yourself by removing the ? from the pattern.

But this approach is not something that we should finally adopt. We should not go the full file read path. For large input files it is not a good idea.

If we go about doing our business line by line, a single pattern may not suffice. We can still apply the pattern without the m modifier in order to clear all the block comments that start and end on the same line. And then on the output of that we can try the trick for multiline pattern search/replacement.

The following code does the first part (except one thing) and writes the output in a file named tmp.txt.

```
infile = File.open 'def.java','r'
outfile = File.open 'tmp.txt','w'
while line = infile.gets
        line = line.gsub(/\/\*.*?\*\//,'')
        outfile.print line
end
infile.close
outfile.close
```

The part that it does not do is for the block comment that has a newline after it. It does not take care of the newline (so an empty line is in the output in place of the first block comment).

```
//Project
Nothing to import

few statements
and   a comment
/* This too
        is a commenting
        //having another comment trapped within
        */
        few more statements
        //Alternatively : instead of good bye you may say
see you
```

To take care of such empty line, we can look for a newline after the end of the block comment (*/)— either immediately after, or with any number of spaces and tabs in between. So our pattern should be /\/*.*?*\/[\s]*\n/. This, however, means that the second block comment (which has non-whitespace characters after it on the same line) will not be matched and replaced. To avoid this, we can apply both filters one after another. The following code does this and achieves the goal.

```
infile = File.open 'def.java','r'
outfile = File.open 'tmp.txt','w'
while line = infile.gets
        line = line.gsub( /\/\*.*?\*\/[\s]*\n/,'')
        line = line.gsub( /\/\*.*?\*\//,'')
        outfile.print line
end
infile.close
outfile.close
```

The `tmp.txt` output file, which should be our input file for the next stage of development, has the following text.

```
//Project
Nothing to import
few statements
and  a comment
/* This too
        is a commenting
        //having another comment trapped within
        */
        few more statements
        //Alternatively : instead of good bye you may say
see you
```

To tackle multiline comments (while reading line by line), we have to first look for the opening pattern (/*) and once we find it, mark a flag, and then look for the closing pattern.

The following code does the job.

```
infile = File.open 'tmp.txt','r'
while line = infile.gets
        if line.match(/\/\*/)
                commentline = true
        end
        print line if (not commentline)
        if commentline
                commentline = false if line.match(/\*\//)
        end
end
infile.close
```

This is the output:

```
//Project
Nothing to import
few statements
and  a comment
        few more statements
        //Alternatively : instead of good bye you may say
see you
```

So far, so good. But what if the multiline comment has some text before the comment (for the opening line) and after the comment (for the closing line)? That is, something like the following as the input file data.

```
abcd
123 /* open
        and
        close */ 456
efgh
```

The current code won't work in this case. We need to print part of the opening and closing lines, not skip them wholly. The following code should work.

```
infile = File.open 'plinecmt.txt','r'
while line = infile.gets
     if line.match(/\/\*/)
               commentline = true
               print $`
     end
     print line if (not commentline)
     if commentline
          if line.match(/\*\//)
                    commentline = false
                    print $'
          end
     end
end
infile.close
```

Predefined $` and $' variables are used to get the part before and after the (last) match, as appropriate.

Putting it together, making it function-based, and making a small change to avoid a newline for the closing comment line, we have the following.

```
def remove_comment(javafilename)
        infile = File.open javafilename,'r'
        outfile = File.open 'tmp.txt','w'
        while line = infile.gets
```

```
                  line = line.gsub( /\/\*.*?\*\/[\s]*\n/,'')
                  line = line.gsub( /\/\*.*?\*\//,'')
                  outfile.print line
        end
        infile.close
        outfile.close

        infile = File.open 'tmp.txt','r'
        outfile = File.open javafilename,'w'
        while line = infile.gets
            if line.match(/\/\*/)
                    commentline = true
                    outfile.print $`
            end
            outfile.print line if (not commentline)
            if commentline
                    if line.match(/\*\//)
                            commentline = false
                            endpart = $'
                            endpart.gsub!(/^[\s]*\n/,'')
                            outfile.print endpart
                    end
            end
        end
        infile.close
        outfile.close
end

remove_comment('def.java')
```

Notice this part.

```
            if line.match(/\*\//)
                    commentline = false
                    endpart = $'
                    endpart.gsub!(/^[\s]*\n/,'')
                    outfile.print endpart
            end
```

The end part is being stripped of whitespace and newline (at the end). This removes extra newlines in place of the block comment, should the end part (the part after the comment close marker until the end of the line) consists only of whitespaces and newlines.

The objective for making it function-oriented is to make it easier to be adopted for multiple files.

In the preceding code, replace the line containing the call to the function with the following code.

```
arr = Dir.glob('**/*.java')
arr.each {|filename|
        remove_comment(filename)
}
```

Save and close the file. Run the code. The comments are gone.

8.2 Searching and Replacing in Text Files

Problem

Suppose that a project has a lot of `.sql` files: some define tables and others define procedures. Each of these files may have code for single or multiple tables, or single or multiple procedures. All of them are in the same directory (we discussed how to tackle files from different directories in Recipe 6.6).

When all of those files run against a database in a batch for an existing procedure, the 'create procedure' statement fails, and that creates problem for the whole batch. (For now, do not bother with the database technology.) If, however, each of the creates were replaced with 'create and replace' appropriately, then the procedures already created will be skipped without throwing an error and the batch will continue smoothly.

The task is to replace 'create' with 'create or replace' as appropriate (before the word 'procedure').

Solution

To start, we can work on one file that has one or more create procedure scripts. The file used as input (at least initially) has the following data.

```
--This is a create procedure script
--for a few procedures such as inserProc, deleteProc and modifyProc
/* All the procedures
        work on the tables t_abc and t_def
        and are created with
        create procedure statement */

        create procedure insertProc
                a   numeric,
                b   numeric out
begin
        some code
        some more code
end;
/
```

```
--create procedure delProc
CREATE    procedure deleteProc  -- procedure for deletion
                tbl  varchar2(20)
begin
        some code
        some more code
end;
/


create
        procedure modifyProc
                tbl  varchar2(20)
begin
        some code
        some more code
end;
/

create or replace procedure tranProc
                tbl  varchar2(20)
begin
        some code
        some more code
end;
/
--end of script
```

Consider that in that PL/SQL language, two consecutive dashes indicate a line comment and portions within /* and */ are block comments (including those delimiters). And as far as keywords are concerned, the language is not case sensitive.

If create is replaced with create or replace within a comment, it won't be taken seriously. There are a few points that need to be considered for now, but we may build up as we go along.

- There may be more than one space between the word 'create' and the word 'procedure'.

- There may be newlines between them.

- Keywords are not case sensitive.

- Some create procedures may already have 'create or replace'. (The original developer may have been more thoughtful, for instance.)

The first point could be easily taken care of if we look for a pattern of one or more whitespace characters (which includes tabs) between 'create' and 'procedure'. Adding to that the case insensitivity with keywords, we can try a pattern (with the i modifier) like - /\bcreate[\s]+?procedure\b/i.

Note that this has been made non-greedy. The word boundaries are necessary because we do not want to pick up something like 'non-create procedures'. The words 'create' and 'procedure' have to be whole.

Also it would not work across a newline. Why? Because we will be reading line by line (not the entire file in one shot).

Try the following code.

```
infile = File.open 'crprc.txt','r'
outfile = File.open 'out.txt','w'
while line = infile.gets
        line = line.gsub( /\bcreate[\s]+?procedure\b/i,'create or replace')
        outfile.print line
end
infile.close
outfile.close
```

You will find that it tackled a few cases but could not tackle a few others. It has replaced uppercase letters with lowercase letters (which we can live with, since that would not be an issue for running SQL scripts. **However, it has *not worked across multiple lines* (when the word procedure is in another line).** It worked within comments, but that is OK for our purpose.

As an aside, check the previous recipe in this chapter to see if you can implement a solution for this task, where changes are not made within comments.

Note that it did not adversely affect cases where create or replace was already there (because it was only looking for one or more whitespace characters in between, not other characters), which is good.

It's time to tackle the multiline case. For this we use a smaller data file, input2.txt, which has the following data.

```
create procedure abc
begin
end

create
   procedure def
 begin
 end
```

For this part, we first search for lines that has 'create' (followed optionally by any number of whitespace characters until the end of the line) but not 'procedure'. Once such a line is found, we can flag it, and check if the next line has the word procedure preceded by (optionally) zero or more whitespaces. If such is the case for the next line, then take the preceding part of first line (before 'create'), the succeeding part of second line (after 'procedure'), and join them with 'create or replace procedure' in between. If the second line, however, fails to match an eligible 'procedure', unset the flag (set on encountering the first line) and move on.

The preceding should take care of any multiline affairs. Then another pass can be made with the original code for 'create' and 'procedure' in the same line cases. But this part is already coded, so we can concentrate on the multiline part only for now.

The following code works well for the (multiline) purpose. This is with the assumption that the word procedure occurs in the next line furthest from the word create.

```
infile = File.open 'input2.txt','r'
outfile = File.open 'out.txt','w'
while line = infile.gets
        if line.match(/\bcreate[\s]*$/)
                createline = true
                prematch = $`
                line1 = line
                checklinenum = $. + 1
                next #don't do any more processing for this line
        end
        found = false
        if createline and checklinenum == $. #very next line
                createline = false # reset it anyway
                if line.match(/^[\s]*procedure\b/)
                        postmatch = $'
                        found = true;
                end
                #print for both the lines either way
                if not found
                        outfile.print line1
                        outfile.print line #second line
                else #found
                        outfile.print "#{prematch}create or replace
                        procedure#{postmatch}"
                end
                next
        end
        #it is not the createline or the nextline
        outfile.print line
end

infile.close
outfile.close
```

It produces an out.txt file with the following text.

```
create procedure abc
begin
end
```

```
create or replace procedure def
 begin
 end
```

The $. (a predefined variable that holds the line number of the last line read from the current input file) has been used to ensure that the very next line is dealt with when such is applicable.

Combining the bits, making small changes as necessary, making things function-oriented, and also accounting for multiple .sql files, we have the following.

```
def replace_create(sqlfile)
        infile = File.open sqlfile,'r'
        outfile = File.open 'out.txt','w'
        while line = infile.gets
                if line.match(/\bcreate[\s]*$/)
                        createline = true
                        prematch = $`
                        line1 = line
                        checklinenum = $. + 1
                        next #don't do any more processing for this line
                end
                found = false
                if createline and checklinenum == $. #very next line
                        createline = false # reset it anyway
                        if line.match(/^[\s]*procedure\b/)
                                postmatch = $'
                                found = true;
                        end
                        #print for both the lines either way
                        if not found
                                outfile.print line1
                                outfile.print line #second line
                        else #found
                                outfile.print "#{prematch}create or replace
                                procedure#{postmatch}"
                        end
                        next
                end
                #it is not the createline or the nextline
                outfile.print line
        end

        infile.close
        outfile.close

        #second pass (not multiline case)
        infile = File.open 'out.txt','r'
        outfile = File.open sqlfile,'w'
```

```
        while line = infile.gets
                line = line.gsub( /\bcreate[\s]+?procedure\b/i,'create or
                replace')
                outfile.print line
        end
        infile.close
        outfile.close
end

arr = Dir.glob('*.sql')
arr.each {|filename|
        replace_create(filename)
}
```

It should be working fine.

8.3 Removing Duplicates from a Text File

Problem

You have a new project. It deals with a lot of old SQL codes that do not have proper documentation. When you check the database, you see a lot of tables—some with names like inventory_bak or orders_1. You are pretty sure that a lot of these tables are not in use. You cannot find any ERD or a master table script.

One thing you know for sure is that you have a set of scripts (PL/SQL functions and procedures) that are in active use and that there is an exhaustive list of SQL codes (other than table or index creation, etc.). If only you could find out from these scripts which of the tables (a list of distinct table names) are actively in use. You feel that there are not too many. You could look at these tables to make a reasonably good ERD yourself (or possibly use a reverse-engineering tool).

For the sake of ease, you can easily concatenate all of the .sql files into one. You can work on a copy of this combined file. The main goal is to extract the (distinct) table list.

Solution

In this language, the line comments start with two consecutive dashes (they need not be at the beginning of the line) and the block comments are enclosed within /* and */ (delimiters included).

Keywords are not case sensitive, but table names are not. Also, any table names that occur within comments are not of interest.

The search should focus on other points with respect to the language syntax. A query is usually of the following form.

```
select <column list>
from tbl_a, tbl_b,
        tbl c;
```

or

```
select <column list>
from tbl_a, tbl_b,
        tbl c
where some conditions;
```

For select statements, table names should be between the from keyword and either a semicolon (';') or the where keyword, separated by commas (when more than one), but not necessarily occurring on the same line. However, the name of a single table does not span multiple lines and only has letters (in either case) and an underscore.

The following is one form of an update statement.

```
update tbl_a set
<column value assignments>
from tbl_a, tbl_b
where some conditions;
```

The from part is optional, but if it exists, it is similar to that of the select statement. For insert statements, the forms are as follows.

```
insert into tbl_a (column list) values (value list);
```

or

```
insert into tbl_a values (value list);
```

The keyword into is optional.
For delete statements, the forms are as follows.

```
delete from tbl_a;
```

or

```
delete from tbl_a
where some conditions;
```

In either case, the from keyword is optional.

For update and delete, the first table mentioned is a single one. insert always works on a single table.

There may be subqueries within the where clause, but that too has a form part. You never look at the where part for table names (but you do look at the form part, as well as insert, update, and delete statements, in the first table). However, the form part of subqueries is considered (in this case, the delimiter is either where or closing parenthesis).

For simplification, consider that this language has no table alias concept. Also consider that in the active code (any portion that is not commented), the use of the word from only happens in a from clause. (Of course, it has to be the whole word.)

Words may appear with one or more whitespace in between. A comma (',') in the scope may have zero or more whitespaces on either side. ***Whitespace includes newlines, but you may treat them separately***. For the sake of simplification, consider that a comma appears in the same line after a table name (it may have one or more spaces or tabs, or both). And a semicolon and a closing parenthesis also appear similarly in the same line with the immediately preceding token or keyword. Also, two select, insert, delete, or update statements (or two of any combination of these keywords) do not occur on the same line in uncommented code.

The Technical Problem Specification

We need to look for tokens (table names) and make a distinct list/set of them (and print that to a file). The tokens are themselves case sensitive but other keywords are not. Keeping in mind the possible whitespace separation part as applicable (as discussed earlier), they have to be searched within.

- insert or insert into and '(' or values – single occurrence

- update and set – single occurrence

- delete or delete from and semicolon(;) or where – single occurrence

- from and semicolon(;) or where or ***closing parenthesis*** – single occurrence **or** multiple occurrence separated by commas

Step 1: Remove the Comments

The first step is to remove the comments and possibly create another file, which is the input for further processing. After all, we are only interested in the list of tables, not the final SQL file.

Removing block comments was discussed in an earlier task, so this step won't be repeated here. For the sake of simplicity, in this step, you have a file that has all the block comments removed.

For removing the line comments (from the double dash (--) until the end of the line), the following code is good enough.

```
infile = File.open 'inp1.sql','r'
outfile = File.open 'out.txt','w'
while line = infile.gets
        outfile.print line.sub(/\-\-.*$/,'').sub(/^$\n/,'')
end
infile.close
outfile.close
```

The first substitution function with the /\-\-.*$/ pattern is for removing the line comments .The second substitution, with the /^$\n/ pattern, should remove empty lines (except leaving one empty line at the end of the file in certain cases).

Not having any empty lines between active code parts can greatly help further searches.

Going forward, the output file of this code is the input for the next step, which is devoid of any comments and contains only active code.

Step 2: Remove Optional Keywords

Optional keywords are from after delete and into after insert. If you come to think of it, accommodating them in a regular expressions isn't straightforward. If we get rid of them at this stage, further steps will be smoother.

To develop this step, you can use the following in a file as simple input data.

```
delete FROm abc
another line
DELete def
delete
  from ghi
 INSert    into abc1
insert def1
still another line
insert
 INTO ghi1
```

Take the case of delete and from (insert and into are similar except the words are different).

First, consider single-line case(s) and then take a case where the next line may have the optional keyword.

1. If delete is followed with one or more whitespaces and then the word from in the same line, we have a match. Keep in mind that they have to be complete words and case should be ignored. The /\bdelete\b[\s]+?\bfrom\b/i pattern should work.

2. If the preceding pattern does not match and the line still has the delete keyword, then it is possible that there is no word after delete in that line. Till the end of the line, after delete, it is whitespaces (or no character). In that case, if the first word in the next line is from, then we have a match. In the first line, the /\bdelete\b[\s]*$/i pattern should match. And the very next line (as there should be no empty line in the input file, except possibly in the end) should have the /^[\s]*\bfrom\b[\s]*$/i pattern. In absence of which the match isn't available on that occasion.

On this occasion, we can operate on a string by joining two lines (joining two lines in a normal SQL file should not result in a huge string) and treating them as a single line for pattern replacement. (Consider it another way of doing what has been done for the 'create procedure' case, using $.).

The following code will work for a two-line (delete from) case, but it won't work for single-line cases, which are simpler and can be augmented upon easily.

```
infile = File.open 'inp2.sql','r'
outfile = File.open 'out.txt','w'
while line = infile.gets
        if line.match(/\bdelete\b[\s]*$/i)
                firstlinefound = true
                joinedlines = line
                next #don't do any more processing for this line
        end
        if firstlinefound #for the very next line
                firstlinefound = false # reset it
                if line.match(/^[\s]*\bfrom\b/i)
                        #join this line to the last one
                        joinedlines = joinedlines + line
                        #treat the joined line as a regular line and replace
                        joinedlines = joinedlines.sub(/\bdelete\b[\s]+?\
                        bfrom\b/i ,'delete')
                        outfile.print joinedlines
                        joinedlines = '' #reset joinedlines
                        next #no need to go further down for this line
                else #the overall match for delete from failed in this case
                        #print the last line here
                        #the current line will get printed towards the end
                        of while loop anyway
                        outfile.print joinedlines
                        joinedlines = '' #reset joinedlines
                end
        end
        outfile.print line
end

infile.close
outfile.close
```

After removing some comments and putting it in function form (in such a way that it can be used for the insert into case also), and augmenting it with single line cases, the code is as follows.

```
def remove_optional_multiline(infilename, outfilename, typ)
        if typ == 1 #delete from
                word1 = "delete"
                word2 = "from"
        else
                word1 = "insert"
                word2 = "into"
        end
```

```
pat1 = %r{\b#{word1}\b[\s]*$}i
pat2 = %r{^[\s]*\b#{word2}\b}i
pat3 = %r{\b#{word1}\b[\s]+?\b#{word2}\b}i

infile = File.open infilename,'r'
outfile = File.open outfilename,'w'

while line = infile.gets
    if line.match(pat1)
            firstlinefound = true
            joinedlines = line
            next
    end
    if firstlinefound #for the very next line
            firstlinefound = false # reset it
            if line.match(pat2)
                    joinedlines = joinedlines + line
                    joinedlines = joinedlines.sub(pat3,word1)
                    outfile.print joinedlines
                    joinedlines = ''
                    next
            else #the overall match for delete from failed in
            this case
                    outfile.print joinedlines
                    joinedlines = ''
            end
    end
    outfile.print line
end

infile.close
outfile.close
end

def remove_optional_singleline(infilename, outfilename, typ)
    if typ == 1 #delete from
            word1 = "delete"
            word2 = "from"
    else
            word1 = "insert"
            word2 = "into"
    end

    pat = %r{\b#{word1}\b[\s]+?\b#{word2}\b}i

    infile = File.open infilename,'r'
    outfile = File.open outfilename,'w'
```

```
    while line = infile.gets
          line.sub!(pat,word1)
          outfile.print line
    end

    infile.close
    outfile.close
end

remove_optional_multiline('inp2.sql','tmp1.txt',1)
remove_optional_multiline('tmp1.txt','tmp2.txt',2)
remove_optional_singleline('tmp2.txt','tmp1.txt',1)
remove_optional_singleline('tmp1.txt','out.txt',2)

File.delete('tmp1.txt')
File.delete('tmp2.txt')
```

Two functions have been defined for single-line and multiline cases; they are being called with different arguments. Note that the tmp1.txt and tmp2.txt files are used as intermediate files, which are deleted after the main processing is done.

Note the use of %r while creating the patterns. This is one example:

```
pat1 = %r{\b#{word1}\b[\s]*$}i
```

It is used later in the following line.

```
if line.match(pat1)
```

%r{} is equivalent to // for building patterns. But when using it with modifiers (in this case, I) together with variable substitution (in this case word1), this is much easier than the // construct. For the value of word1 as 'delete', the preceding is effectively /\bdelete\b[\s]*$/i.

Notice also the way two lines are joined for replacement when a successful multiline case is identified.

The output of this code should be the input for the next stage.

Step 3: Collect Tokens

By this stage, the input file is already in good shape. There are no comments, no empty lines (except possibly at the end), and no optional keywords. At this step, the subtask is to collect the tokens (table names) that may occur.

- After the update keyword: single token

- After the insert keyword: single token

- After the delete keyword: single token

- Between the from keyword and the where keyword, or a semicolon or a closing parenthesis: single token or multiple tokens separated by commas

Of course, newline and other whitespace character separation applies.

Note that I did not mention looking between two keywords. For example, I did not specify to look between the update and set keywords. This is because we should be looking for complete words (keywords), and since there is no commented code, the word update can only occur at the beginning of an update statement and nowhere else. So if we just take the very next word, it should be the table name that we are looking for. We need not bother about the set keyword.

Let's look at the first three cases. The update statement is the test case for development. Take the following code.

```
def print_tblnm(infilename, outfilename, word)
        infile = File.open infilename,'r'
        outfile = File.open outfilename,'w'

        pat1 = %r{\b#{word}\b[\s]*$}i
        pat2 = %r{\b#{word}\b[\s]+?(\b[\w]+\b)}i

        firstlinefound = false
        while line = infile.gets
                if line.match(pat1) #two line case
                        firstlinefound = true
                        joinedlines = line
                        next
                end
                if firstlinefound #second line for two line case
                        firstlinefound = false
                        #take the first word
                        matched = line.match(/^[\s]*?(\b[\w]+\b)/)
                        tbl_name = matched.captures[0]
                        outfile.puts tbl_name
                        next
                end
                #at this point it is neither first line nor second line
                #for two line case, but may be a single line case
                if matched = line.match(pat2)
                        tbl_name = matched.captures[0]
                        outfile.puts tbl_name
                end

        end
        infile.close
        outfile.close
end

print_tblnm('upd.sql','output.txt','update')
```

The input file contains the following data.

```
update abc set
a line
update Def
        set a =
another line
updATE
        Efg  set b =
last line
```

The following output data is produced.

```
abc
Def
Efg
```

This is fine.

Now let's look at the fourth case: between the from keyword and the where keyword, or a semicolon or a closing parenthesis, a single token or multiple tokens separated by commas, and assume that no two from keywords occur on the same line. Take the following data as input.

```
from abc where
from abc,def where
one line
FROM def  ,
        ghi, abc1 where abc1.a in (
        some select from
  abc2, abc3) data
        another line
from def1
        def2,
        def3 ;
from def2, ghi2;
last line
```

Use the following code.

```
def print_tblnm_from(infilename, outfilename)
        infile = File.open infilename,'r'
        outfile = File.open outfilename,'w'

        firstlinefound = false
        joinedlines = ''
        while line = infile.gets
                if line.match(/\bfrom\b/i)
```

```
                           # serach if terminator is also in the same line
                           after from
                           postmatch = $'
                           if postmatch.match(/(;|\)|\bwhere\b)/i) #terminates
                           in the same line
                                   #print the tablename part
                                   matched = line.match(/\bfrom\b(.*)(;|\)|\
                                   bwhere\b)/i)
                                   outfile.puts matched.captures[0]
                           else #multiline case - keep adding lines till
                           terminator is found
                                   joinedlines = line.chomp
                                   firstlinefound = true
                                   next
                           end
                 end
                 if firstlinefound #second line onwards for multiline case
                         joinedlines = joinedlines + line.chomp
                         if line.match(/(;|\)|\bwhere\b)/i) #terminator line
                         found
                                   #do the extraction and reset
                                   matched = joinedlines.match(/\bfrom\b(.*)
                                   (;|\)|\bwhere\b)/i)
                                   outfile.puts matched.captures[0]
                                   firstlinefound = false;
                                   next
                         else
                                   next #line already added - look in the next
                                   line
                         end
                 end
                 #at this point it is not a line of interest

        end
        infile.close
        outfile.close
end

print_tblnm_from('from.txt','output.txt')
```

A somewhat crude table list is printed in the output file.

```
abc
abc,def
def, ghi, abc1
 abc2, abc3
def1 def2, def3
def2, ghi2
```

Note that the preceding code keeps concatenating lines (for multiline cases) until the terminator is found (including the terminator line). And once the whole set (for that occasion of from keyword) is joined, the extraction is done.

Step 4: Get Distinct Values

Finally, we come up with a file that has the table names but is not distinct. It is somewhat in the form of the following data.

```
Abc
AAbc
abc1
EFg
ghGhi
 abc
 abc, def
 def, ghi, abc1
  abc2, abc3
 def1 def2, def3
 def2, ghi2
```

The next subtask is to get a list of distinct table names from this data. This is rather easy compared to what has already been done. The following code works.

```ruby
require 'set'

set = Set.new

infile = File.open 'mixed.txt','r'
while line = infile.gets
        line1 = line.gsub(',','')
        #print line
        line2 = line1.gsub(/[\s]+/,' ')
        arr = line2.split
        arr.each {|tblnm| set.add(tblnm)}
end
infile.close

outfile = File.open 'output.txt','w'
set.each {|tblnm| outfile.puts tblnm}
outfile.close
```

It produces this:

```
Abc
AAbc
abc1
EFg
```

```
ghGhi
abc
def
ghi
abc2
abc3
def1
def2
def3
ghi2
```

A set has been used here to get a distinct list of tables. Note the following lines.

```
require 'set'
set = Set.new
        arr.each {|tblnm| set.add(tblnm)}
set.each {|tblnm| outfile.puts tblnm}
```

All of the lines relate to set. The second line creates a new set. The third line's code adds elements. The fourth line's code is iteration over the elements.

You may try to properly combine all of these steps, with appropriate modifications, to get the desired list of tables.

8.4 Reading XML as Text

Problem

XML in Ruby can be parsed as XML. There are toolkits and APIs such as 'REXML' or 'nokogiri' available for it. However this demonstration uses Ruby and regular expressions to parse and process XML data as if it were a text file.

In certain situations, it may be helpful to parse an XML file as a text file. One possible case may be when an element with a particular tag name is deep within the XML structure, occurring maybe only a few times in the entire XML file. Trying to get the value of the element (in each occurrence) through XML parsing and Xpath expressions could be quite time-consuming to code when compared to simple text filtering.

Solution

The following is the XML data in a file named invoice.xml.

```
<?xml version="1.0"?>
<invoice>
        <purchase_date>14/10/2013</purchase_date>
        <customer>
                <id>1</id>
                <name>John Doe</name>
                <address>15 Downing Street, NSW 2130</address>
        </customer>
```

211

```
<items>
        <item>
                <name>trousers</name>
                <qty>1</qty>
                <price>20.00</price>
        </item>
        <item>
                <name>shirt</name>
                <qty>4</qty>
                <price>15.00</price>
        </item>
        <item>
                <name>socks</name>
                <qty>2</qty>
                <price>10.00</price>
        </item>
    </items>
</invoice>
```

The task is to find out—using a Ruby script—the total amount of the invoice.
The following code will work.

```
def getval(line,tag)
        pat = '<' + tag + '>(.*)<\/' + tag + '>'
        if matched = line.match(pat)
                return matched.captures[0]
        end
end

total = 0

infile = File.open('invoice.xml','r')
while (line = infile.gets)
        tag = 'qty'
        val = getval(line,tag)
        quantity = val.to_f unless val.nil?

        tag = 'price'
        val = getval(line,tag)
        if !val.nil?
                price = val.to_f
                total = total + quantity * price
        end
end
infile.close

print "Total : #{total}"
```

Note that the getval function returns the value of a tag (provided the whole tag is in a single line) or nil, given the line and the tag string as input. This is a very useful function for analyzing these kinds of XML files. For instance, if you wanted to find the price of an item (say, a shirt) you could have used the following code (again using the same function).

```
def getval(line,tag)
        pat = '<' + tag + '>(.*)<\/' + tag + '>'
        if matched = line.match(pat)
                return matched.captures[0]
        end
end

infile = File.open('invoice.xml','r')
while (line = infile.gets)
        tag = 'name'
        val = getval(line,tag)
        item_name = val unless val.nil?

        tag = 'price'
        val = getval(line,tag)
        if !val.nil? and item_name.eql?('shirt')
                price = val
                print "Price of a shirt is #{price}"
        end
end
infile.close
```

It works fine and prints as follows.

```
Price of a shirt is 15.00
```

Note that even if you change the name of the customer to shirt, the program still provides the correct price for a shirt. This is because it works on the item_name, which is the value of the last name element picked up at the time that it is looking for price— so the name of the customer is overridden by the time it reaches the first price tag.

8.5 A Case for Hash Buckets

Problem

You have been given a transaction file (named tran.txt) with the following content.

```
032349,game purchase,01/09/16,30.35,CR
045678,shopping,01/09/16,55.40,CR
045678,refund of ticket,03/09/16,60.50,DR
023541,restaurant bill,03/09/16,56.55,CR
```

```
032349,weekly salary,03/09/16,2349.80,DR
023541,movie ticket,04/09/16,45.00,CR
032349,cash deposit,05/09/16,200.00,DR
032349,laptop purchase,05/09/16,2549.50,CR
045678,withdrawal from ATM,05/09/16,250.00,CR
023541,sale of books,08/09/16,300.00,DR
```

It is a comma-separated file in which the columns are account number, description of transaction, date, amount, and DR or CR (denoting whether the transaction is debit or credit; debit is positive for the account, credit is negative).

There is no data anomaly (all rows are valid data). All the accounts have an initial balance of zero. The task is to write a program, which will process the transactions in the accounts and then come up with the (final) balances of the accounts.

Solution

The following code will work.

```
Tran = Struct.new(:acctno, :amount)
tranarr = []
i = 0
infile = File.open 'tran.txt','r'
while (line = infile.gets)
        arr = line.chomp.split(',')
        acctno = arr[0]
        amount = arr[3].to_f
        if (arr[4] == "CR")
                amount *= -1
        end
        tranarr[i] = Tran.new(acctno,amount)
        i += 1
end
infile.close

h = Hash.new

tranarr.each { |tran|
        acct = tran.acctno
        amt = tran.amount
        firsttime = h[acct].nil?
        if firsttime
                h[acct] = amt
        else
                h[acct] = h[acct] + amt
        end
}
```

```
h.each { |k,v|
        fmtamt = "%.02f" % v.round(2)
        puts "balance of account #{k} is #{fmtamt}"
}
```

It generates the following output.

```
balance of account 032349 is -30.05
balance of account 045678 is -244.90
balance of account 023541 is 198.45
```

How It Works

Note the following about this file.

- It uses struct, split, string formatting, and nil check of objects, among other things.

- It also uses iterator each.

- The struct is defined minimally, with only two fields that are really needed. Determining whether the amount is positive or negative is calculated prior to putting it in the struct.

- The hash is used as a holder of different accounts. When there is already a balance available for the account, it is updated with the current amount; otherwise, the amount is freshly put (as if it is the first entry in the account). Hash is ideal in such situations.

This solution concept can be generalized to address many tasks that require similar bucketing.

APPENDIX A

■ ■ ■

Solutions to Exercises

Solutions for Chapter 1

(Solution) Excercise 1.1

```
sum = 0
for i in 1..10
        sum = sum + i * i
end
puts sum
```

(Solution) Excercise 1.2

```
sum = 1
for i in 1..6
        sum = sum * i
end
puts sum
```

(Solution) Excercise 1.3

```
a = 0
b = 1
for i in 1..10
        c = a + b
        puts c
        a = b
        b = c
end
```

© Malay Mandal 2016
M. Mandal, *Ruby Recipes*, DOI 10.1007/978-1-4842-2469-4

Solutions for Chapter 2

(Solution) Excercise 2.1

```
infile = File.open('lnsize.txt','r')
max = -1
maxln = ''
while (line = infile.gets)
        size = line.chomp.size
        if max < size
                max = size
                maxln = line
        end
end
infile.close
puts maxln
puts max
```

(Solution) Excercise 2.2

```
infile = File.open('palin.txt','r')
while (line = infile.gets)
        x = line.chomp.downcase.gsub(' ','')
        y = x.reverse
        if (x == y)
                puts 'A palindrome : ' + line.chomp
        else
                puts 'Not a palindrome : ' + line.chomp
        end
end
infile.close
```

Solutions for Chapter 3

(Solution) Excercise 3.1

```
def fibo(n)
  if n == 0
        0
  elsif n == 1
    1
  else
    fibo(n-1) + fibo(n-2)
  end
end
puts fibo(8)
```

(Solution) Excercise 3.2

```
i = 1
i += 1 until i * i > 1000
puts i-1
```

(Solution) Excercise 3.3

```
sum = 0
for i in 1...100
  sum += i if ((i % 15) > 0) and ((i % 3) == 0 || (i % 5) == 0)
end
puts sum
```

Solutions for Chapter 4

(Solution) Excercise 4.1

```
def canformword(arr,word)
        arrword = word.chars
        arrleft = arr
        flag = true
        for i in 0...arrword.size
                ch = arrword[i]
                if !arrleft.include?(ch)
                        flag = false
                        break
                else
                        ind = arrleft.index(ch)
                        arrleft.delete_at(ind)
                end
        end
        if flag
                puts 'can form word'
        else
                puts 'can not form word'
        end
end

canformword(['y','z','b','e','a','u','t'], 'beauty')
canformword(['r','o','u','g','h'], 'tough')
```

(Solution) Excercise 4.2

```ruby
def timeinmin(tm)
        a = tm.split(':')
        a[0].to_i * 60 + a[1].to_i
end

def gethashfromfile(filename)
        thefile = File.open(filename,'r')
        h = Hash.new
        while (line = thefile.gets)
                x = line.chomp.split(/\s+/)
                h[x[0]] = timeinmin(x[1])
        end
        thefile.close
        h
end

h1 = gethashfromfile('arrtime.txt')
h2 = gethashfromfile('deptime.txt')

k1 = h1.keys
k2 = h2.keys

kcommon = k1 & k2
knotinboth = (k1 - kcommon) | (k2 - kcommon)

arr = kcommon.to_a
for i in 0...arr.size
        stay = h2[arr[i]] - h1[arr[i]]
        if stay < 0
                puts arr[i] + ': data issue'
        else
                puts arr[i] + ': stay ' + stay.to_s + ' minutes'
        end
end

arr2 = knotinboth.to_a
for i in 0...arr2.size
        puts arr2[i] + ': data issue'
end
```

Solutions for Chapter 5

(Solution) Excercise 5.1

```
h = {
        "Abani Sen" => 650,
        "Dora Pridle" => 573,
        "Sana Chowdhury" => 824,
        "Pritish Panda" => 732
        }

h.each { |k, v|
    str = ''
        str = ' : First Division' if v > 599
        puts "#{k} : Marks obtained #{v}#{str}"
}
```

(Solution) Excercise 5.2

```
h = {
        "Abani Sen" => 650,
        "Dora Pridle" => 573,
        "Sana Chowdhury" => 824,
        "Pritish Panda" => 732
        }

arr = h.invert.sort{|a,b| b<=>a}

arr.each { |x|
        str = ''
        str = ' : First Division' if x[0] > 599
        puts "#{x[1]} : Marks obtained #{x[0]}#{str}"
}
```

(Solution) Excercise 5.3

```
h = {
        "Abani Sen" => 650,
        "Dora Pridle" => 573,
        "Sana Chowdhury" => 824,
        "Pritish Panda" => 732
        }
```

```
h.map {|k,v|
        case v
        when 0..500
                puts "#{k} : no credit"
        when 501..600
                puts "#{k} : credit : 10"
        when 601..700
                puts "#{k} : credit : 20"
        when 701..800
                puts "#{k} : credit : 40"
        else
                puts "#{k} : credit : 70"
        end
}
```

Solutions for Chapter 7

(Solution) Excercise 7.1

```
sen1 = "Abani Sen mentioned that he will be absent on Thursday."
sen2 = "The president of USA, Barrack Obama, proposed the bill."

def getname(sent)
        if matched = sent.match(/([A-Z]\w+)\s+([A-Z]\w+)/)
                a = matched.captures
                puts "name : #{a[0]} #{a[1]}"
        end
end

getname(sen1)
getname(sen2)
```

(Solution) Excercise 7.2

```
infile = File.open('train.log','r')
while (line1 = infile.gets)
        line = line1.chomp
        if matched = line.match(/^Train (.*) (departed|arrived) (from|at)
        (.*) station (.*)$/)
                a = matched.captures
                puts "train : #{a[0]} #{a[1]} station : #{a[3]} time :
                #{a[4]}"
        end
end
infile.close
```

Index

© Malay Mandal 2016
M. Mandal, *Ruby Recipes*, DOI 10.1007/978-1-4842-2469-4

Get the eBook for only $4.99!

Why limit yourself?

Now you can take the weightless companion with you wherever you go and access your content on your PC, phone, tablet, or reader.

Since you've purchased this print book, we are happy to offer you the eBook for just $4.99.

Convenient and fully searchable, the PDF version enables you to easily find and copy code—or perform examples by quickly toggling between instructions and applications.

To learn more, go to http://www.apress.com/us/shop/companion or contact support@apress.com.

Apress®
THE EXPERT'S VOICE™

Printed in the United States
By Bookmasters